Jelly Roll
SAMPLER QUILTS

Jelly Roll
SAMPLER QUILTS

10 stunning sampler quilts to
make from over 50 patchwork blocks

PAM & NICKY LINTOTT

D&C
David and Charles
www.rucraft.co.uk

A DAVID & CHARLES BOOK
Copyright © David & Charles Limited 2011

David & Charles is an F+W Media Inc. company
4700 East Galbraith Road, Cincinnati, OH 45236

First published in the UK and US in 2011

Text and designs copyright © Pam and Nicky Lintott 2011
Layout and photography copyright © David & Charles 2011

Pam and Nicky Lintott have asserted their right to be identified as authors
of this work in accordance with the Copyright, Designs and Patents Act, 1988.

A catalogue record for this book is available from the British Library.

ISBN-13: 978-0-7153-3844-5 paperback
ISBN-10: 0-7153-3844-7 paperback

Printed in China by RR Donnelley
for David & Charles
Brunel House   Newton Abbot   Devon

Acquisitions Editor Cheryl Brown
Editor James Brooks
Project Editor Lin Clements
Design Manager Sarah Clark
Photographers Sian Irvine, Marie Absolom, Joe Giacomet and Karl Adamson
Production Controller Kelly Smith

David & Charles publish high quality books on a wide range of subjects. For
more great book ideas visit: **www.rucraft.co.uk**

CONTENTS

Introduction   6

Getting Started   8

Important Techniques   10

Block Library   12

Classic Sampler Quilt   **14**

Big and Bold Sampler Quilt   **34**

Snowball Sampler Quilt   **46**

Star Sampler Quilt   **72**

Basket Sampler Quilt   **88**

Pick 'n' Mix Quilts   **102**

Fruit Salad Quilt   104

Liquorice Sticks Quilt   108

Rhubarb and Custard Quilt   110

Peppermint Whirls Quilt   112

A Quarter of… Quilt   116

General Techniques   120

Acknowledgments   127

About the Authors   127

Useful Contacts   127

Index   128

INTRODUCTION

We all love the quick and easy quilts that can be made from Jelly Rolls™ with 2½in wide strips ready cut for us to just sit down and sew. It is easy to forget how magical it is to be able to hold forty *different* fabrics in the palm of your hand. Imagine staggering around a quilt shop with forty bolts of fabric and then seeing the face of the assistant when you ask for a 2½in wide strip or the smallest piece available from each bolt please!

So many beginners start their quilting journey with a sampler quilt. Traditionally, these quilts feature a number of different blocks in an arrangement that shows the skill of the maker in coping with different techniques. They are rewarding to make because they offer the opportunity to build skills. The blocks can be a mixture or can follow a theme. We have chosen to base our Jelly Roll™ sampler quilts around five themes:

Classic Sampler Quilt – there are twelve gorgeous blocks in this quilt, focussing on well-loved designs that have stood the test of time.

Big and Bold Sampler Quilt – five distinctive blocks in this striking quilt are linked by connector blocks, making this colourful quilt easy to sew.

Snowball Sampler Quilt – the eighteen bright and sunny blocks in this quilt are linked by snowball blocks, creating a contemporary design.

Star Sampler Quilt – there are three different sizes of star blocks in this elegant quilt, radiating out from a central star.

Basket Sampler Quilt – nine different basket blocks in fresh blues and whites were used to create this lovely quilt, set on point for extra impact.

For many quilters, especially beginners, the biggest problem is choosing the fabrics for a sampler quilt. So, how great would it be if we could harness the array of fabrics available in a Jelly Roll™ to create a gorgeous scrappy sampler quilt? Well, it can be done. The strips from a Jelly Roll™ can be utilized in this way and in this book we show you how. We give you five different sampler quilts with five variations, containing over fifty different blocks in different sizes, all showing exactly the number of strips required to make each block. Each quilt can be made from just *one* Jelly Roll™.

And that's not all! Not only do we give you instructions for making over fifty blocks for sampler quilts, we also show you how to 'pick and mix' to create quilts using just a few chosen blocks. Understanding how versatile these blocks are will help you create your own unique quilts, choosing the blocks that you like and want to experiment with. Rotary cutting instructions are included to enable even a beginner to get started on their first sampler quilt. We hope this book will be the start of an exciting quilting journey for you.

The blocks in our sampler quilts use just one Jelly Roll™, with extra fabric required for sashings and borders. Be guided by what is in your Jelly Roll™ and be flexible. If you like a safety net, consider having a long quarter of a coordinating light and dark fabric to hand when you start your quilt. It may just give you that extra bit of confidence when sorting your strips to know you have a few extra strips to play with.

GETTING STARTED...

WHAT IS A JELLY ROLL?

A Jelly Roll™ is a roll of forty fabrics cut in 2½in wide strips across the width of the fabric. Moda introduced Jelly Rolls™ to showcase new fabric ranges. How inspirational to have one 2½in wide strip of each new fabric wrapped up so deliciously! Our thanks go to Moda for inspiring us and allowing us to use the name Jelly Roll™ in our book.

If you want to make any of the quilts in this book and don't have a Jelly Roll™ to use, then cut a 2½in wide strip across the width of the fabric from forty fabrics from your stash. We know Jelly Rolls™ look so gorgeous you don't like to unroll them – they are an art form in themselves – however they make great quilts too! Go on, untie the ribbon and be inspired by forty different coordinating fabrics. Just flick through these pages and see the quilts you can make with *just one roll*!

IMPERIAL OR METRIC?

Jelly Rolls™ from Moda are cut 2½in wide and at The Quilt Room we have continued to cut our strip bundles 2½in wide. When quilt making, it is impossible to mix metric and imperial measurements. It would be absurd to have a 2½in strip and tell you to cut it 6cm to make a square! It wouldn't be square and nothing would fit. This caused a dilemma when writing instructions for our quilts and a decision had to be made. All our instructions therefore are written in inches. To convert inches to centimetres, multiply the inch measurement by 2.54. For your convenience, any additional fabric you need, noted in the Requirements panel at the start of the quilt instructions, is given in both metric and imperial.

SEAM ALLOWANCE

We cannot stress enough the importance of maintaining an accurate scant ¼in seam allowance throughout. Please take the time to check your seam allowance – see Seam Allowance Test, in the Important Techniques section.

QUILT SIZE

In this book the quilts show what can be achieved with just one Jelly Roll™. Additional fabric is used for sashings, borders and bindings but the basis of each quilt is just one Jelly Roll™. If you want to make a larger version of any quilt you can calculate your extra requirements quite easily as each block shows how many strips are required.

DIAGRAMS

Diagrams have been provided to assist you and these are normally beneath or beside the relevant stepped instruction. The direction in which fabric should be pressed is indicated by arrows on the diagrams. The reverse side of the fabric is usually shown in a lighter colour than the right side.

SORTING STRIPS

Our sorting instructions will tell you exactly how many strips or parts of a strip you need for each block. In order not to waste any fabric, this can be as little as a quarter strip. Our calculations are based on a strip being 42in long, so a quarter strip measurement is 10½in long, a half strip is 21in long and a three-quarter strip is 31½in long.

WASHING NOTES

It is important that pre-cut strips are *not* washed before use as they could distort. Save the washing until your quilt is complete and then make use of a colour catcher in the wash or possibly dry clean the quilt.

IMPORTANT TECHNIQUES

We had so many blocks to put into this book we felt giving these important techniques at the beginning would not only make an easy reference point but also give us more space for blocks and quilts. All the blocks in our sampler quilts are formed from squares, rectangles, half-square triangle units, quarter-square triangles and rectangles with flip-over corners (flying geese units). These instructions need to be referred to when making the blocks. If you are using a speciality ruler other than the Multi-Size 45/90 please make sure you are cutting on the correct lines. The Multi-Size 45/90 shows the *finished size* markings so if you are using another ruler do check before cutting. General techniques are described at the end of the book.

MAKING HALF-SQUARE TRIANGLE UNITS WITH THE MULTI-SIZE 45/90 RULER

1 Take a dark strip and a light strip and press right sides together, ensuring that they are exactly one on top of the other. The pressing will help hold the two strips together.

2 Lay the strips out on a cutting mat and position the Multi-Size 45/90 as shown in the diagram, lining up the 2in mark at the bottom edge of the strips. Trim the selvedge and cut the first triangle. You will notice that the cut out triangle has a flat top. This would just have been a dog ear you needed to cut off so it's saving you time!

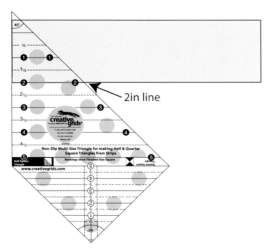

3 Rotate the ruler180 degrees as shown in the diagram and cut the next triangle. Continue along the strip, alternating in this way to cut the required number of triangles.

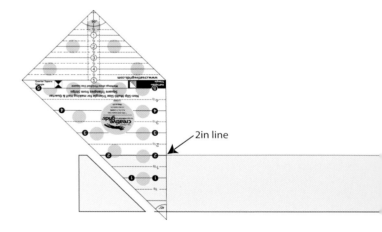

4 Keep the two triangles right sides together, pinning if desired. Using a ¼in seam, sew along the diagonal to form a half-square triangle unit. Trim all dog ears and press open with the seams pressed towards the darker fabric. These half-square triangles will make a 2in finished unit.

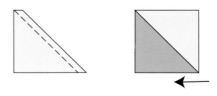

MAKING QUARTER-SQUARE TRIANGLES WITH THE MULTI-SIZE 45/90 RULER

1 Position the Multi-Size 45/90 on the fabric strip, as shown in the diagram below, lining up the 4in marker line with the bottom of the strip. Cut either side of the ruler to form one triangle.

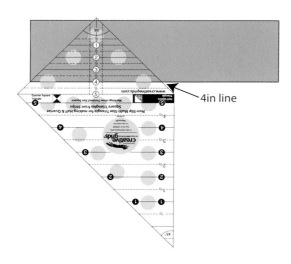

2 Rotate the ruler 180 degrees and cut another triangle. Continue along the strip in this way to cut the required number of triangles.

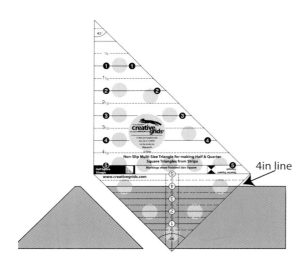

3 Pin two triangles right sides together. Using a ¼in seam, sew along the side. Repeat this with two more triangles.

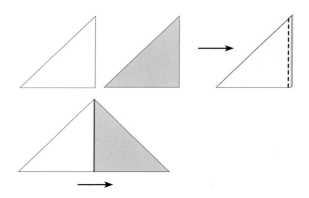

4 Pin the two triangle units together, aligning the centre neatly. Sew together and press open. These quarter-square triangles will make a 4in finished square.

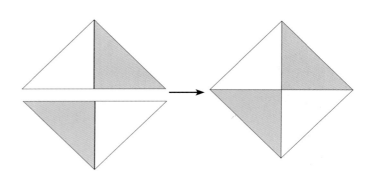

MAKING FLYING GEESE UNITS

1 These flying geese units are made with flip-over corners. Take a 2½in square allocated to make the flip-over corner and lay it right sides together on a rectangle. Sew across the diagonal. If it helps, draw the diagonal line in first or make a fold to mark your stitching line.

2 Flip the square over and press towards the corner. Trim the excess fabric from the corner square but do not trim the excess fabric from the rectangle as, although this creates a little more bulk, it does help to keep your work in shape. Repeat on the other side to create a flying geese unit.

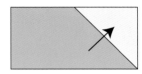

SEAMS

We cannot stress enough the importance of maintaining an accurate ¼in seam allowance throughout when making a quilt. We prefer to say an accurate *scant* ¼in seam because there are two factors to take into consideration. First, the thickness of thread and second, when you press your seam allowance to one side, it takes up a tiny amount of fabric. These are both extremely small amounts but if they are ignored you will find your *exact* ¼in seam allowance is taking up more than ¼in.

SEAM ALLOWANCE TEST

It is well worth testing your seam allowance before starting on a quilt and most sewing machines have various needle positions which can be used to make any adjustments.

Take a 2½in strip and cut off three segments each 1½in wide (diagram A). Sew two segments together down the longer side and press the seam to one side. Sew the third segment across the top – it should fit exactly. If it doesn't, you need to make an adjustment to your seam allowance. If it is too long, your seam allowance is too wide and can be corrected by moving the needle on your sewing machine to the right. If it is too small, your seam allowance is too narrow and this can be corrected by moving the needle to the left.

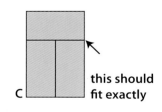

A   B   C   **this should fit exactly**

8IN BLOCKS

Eccentric Star (Snowball Sampler)

Windblown Square (Snowball Sampler)

Sawtooth Star (Snowball Sampler)

Fan (Snowball Sampler)

Marsha Washington Star (Snowball Sampler)

Stardust (Star Sampler)

10IN BLOCKS

May Basket (Basket Sampler)

Floral Basket (Basket Sampler)

12IN BLOCKS

Tulip (Classic Sampler)

Rocky Road (Classic Sampler)

Card Trick (Classic Sampler)

Maple Star (Classic Sampler)

Amish Star (Star Sampler)

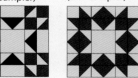
Love in the Mist (Star Sampler)

16IN BLOCKS

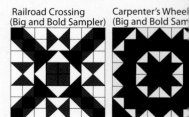

Railroad Crossing (Big and Bold Sampler)

Carpenter's Wheel (Big and Bold Sam...)

BLOCK LIBRARY

There are 55 different blocks in this book, in varying sizes, all shown here. This library shows you the wide choice available to you, which will not only allow you to create the exciting quilts shown in the book but also to pick blocks to create quilt designs of your own. The Pick 'n' Mix section shows some examples.

Spinning Stars
(Snowball Sampler)

Friendship Star
(Snowball Sampler)

King's Crown
(Snowball Sampler)

Buckeye Beauty
(Snowball Sampler)

Spinner
(Snowball Sampler)

Flying Dutchman
(Snowball Sampler)

Fox and Cheese
(Snowball Sampler)

Water Wheel
(Snowball Sampler)

Snowball
(Snowball Sampler)

Quartet
(Snowball Sampler)

Shaded Trail
(Snowball Sampler)

Nelson's Victory
(Snowball Sampler)

Geese in Flight
(Snowball Sampler)

Evening Star
(Snowball Sampler)

Hanging Basket
(Basket Sampler)

Cherry Basket
(Basket Sampler)

Sewing Basket
(Basket Sampler)

Fruit Basket
(Basket Sampler)

Bread Basket
(Basket Sampler)

Picnic Basket
(Basket Sampler)

Tulip Basket
(Basket Sampler)

Star Choice
(Classic Sampler)

Rolling Stone
(Classic Sampler)

Rolling Pinwheel
(Classic Sampler)

Union Square
(Classic Sampler)

Spiral
(Classic Sampler)

Garden Trail
(Classic Sampler)

Arrowhead
(Classic Sampler)

Streak of Lightning
(Classic Sampler)

Crow's Foot
(Star Sampler)

Rising Star
(Star Sampler)

Cup and Saucers
(Star Sampler)

Eddystone Light
(Star Sampler)

Indian Hatchet
(Star Sampler)

Japanese Star
(Big and Bold Sampler)

Chequered Star
(Big and Bold Sampler)

Blackford Beauty
(Big and Bold Sampler)

Connector Block
(Big and Bold Sampler)

Twinkling Star
(Star Sampler)

CLASSIC
SAMPLER QUILT

So many beginners start their quilting journey by making a classic sampler quilt. The beauty of using a Jelly Roll™ for this type of quilt is that you know the fabrics are going to coordinate, so you can concentrate on making flawless blocks. With a designer collection of fabrics you also know the result is going to be stunning.

Our classic quilt includes some really traditional blocks, such as Card Trick, Maple Star and Streak of Lightning, and a few you may not be so familiar with but are easy to piece. We made the quilt with 12in blocks in a Moda Blackbird Design range, Garden Party, which is typical of their gentle country look – soft blues, pinks and greens with lots of cream and tan. Our variation, shown at the end of this chapter, was made using a totally different Jelly Roll™ by April Cornell – very spring like with yellows and blues. Be inspired by your Jelly Roll™ and off you go.

CLASSIC SAMPLER QUILT

VITAL STATISTICS

QUILT SIZE	52in x 66in
BLOCK SIZE	12in square
BLOCKS PER QUILT	12
SETTING	3 x 4 blocks + 2in wide sashing and 4in wide border

REQUIREMENTS

- One Jelly Roll™
- 32in (80cm) of sashing fabric
- 32in (80cm) of border fabric
- 20in (50cm) of binding fabric
- Multi-Size 45/90 or other speciality ruler for making half-square and quarter-square triangles

SORTING YOUR JELLY ROLL STRIPS

- Sort your strips before you start your quilt. Each block gives its own strip requirements but it is important to sort them before you start your quilt and label the strips once sorted. You can change anything around and mediums can become darks or lights depending on the other strips chosen so be prepared to play around with them until you are happy with the results.
- *Important*: when you need more than one strip for a colour, i.e., one and a half strips for the medium B in Block 1, you need to make sure you choose those that look similar. You don't want one strip of a medium green and a half strip of a pink. Select one strip of a medium green and then a half strip of another medium green. Our cutting chart overleaf gives the strips required for each block and will help you sort the strips.
- *Important*: don't discard any offcuts from the Jelly Roll™ strips when making the blocks as the offcuts are needed for Block 12 and also for the sashing squares. We have allowed plenty of fabric for the blocks so you will have sufficient.

CUTTING INSTRUCTIONS

Sashing fabric:
- Cut eleven 2½in strips across the width of the fabric and subcut each strip into three rectangles each 2½in x 12½in. You need thirty-one (two are spare).

Border fabric:
- Cut six 4½in strips across the width of the fabric.

Binding fabric:
- Cut six 2½in strips across the width of the fabric.

CUTTING CHART FOR THE CLASSIC SAMPLER QUILT

When looking at the strip requirements for each block, the medium/dark/light strips are only for your guidance and you can use whatever you prefer to make your quilt unique to you. The colours given are the colours we have used in our Garden Party version of the quilt described in the instructions. It is important to select all your strips at the start.

As you can see from the table below, a total of forty-one strips is needed for the quilt but there are plenty of offcuts to complete Block 12, so don't panic! Offcuts are also used to make the sashing squares so it is important that you *do not discard any fabric* when making your blocks.

BLOCK	MEDIUM A STRIPS	MEDIUM B STRIPS	DARK STRIPS	LIGHT STRIPS	TOTAL STRIPS
1 Tulip	1 gold	1½ blue	1 brown		**3½**
2 Rocky Road	½ blue	1 pink	½ brown	1 cream	**3**
3 Star Choice	½ brown		1 green	2 cream	**3½**
4 Rolling Stone	1½ pink	1½ blue	½ brown		**3½**
5 Rolling Pinwheel	½ pink		1 brown	2 cream	**3½**
6 Union Square	1½ green	1 pink		1 cream	**3½**
7 Spiral	1½ pink	½ blue	1 brown	1½ grey	**4½**
8 Garden Trail	2 gold	1½ green	½ brown		**4**
9 Card Trick	1 green		1 brown	1 cream	**3**
10 Maple Star	1½ blue	½ gold	1 brown		**3**
11 Arrowhead	1 pink	½ blue	1 brown	1 cream	**3½**
12 Streak of Lightning	½	½ med blue ½ med C	½	½	**2½**
TOTAL STRIPS	**13**	**9**	**9**	**10**	**41**

MAKING BLOCK 1 – TULIP

TOTAL STRIPS = 3½
- 1 colour A medium strip (gold).
- 1½ colour B medium strips (blue).
- 1 colour C dark strip (brown).

CUTTING INSTRUCTIONS
- Colour A – from one strip cut:
  four 2½in x 4½in rectangles,
  four 2½in squares,
  one 2½in x 14in rectangle.
- Colour B – from one and a half strips cut:
  two 2½in x 14in rectangles,
  twelve 2½in squares.
- Colour C – from one strip cut:
  one 2½in x 14in rectangle,
  four 2½in squares.

MAKING THE HALF-SQUARE TRIANGLE UNITS

1 Take a colour A 14in rectangle and a colour B 14in rectangle and, referring to the Important Techniques section, cut eight sets of triangles using the Multi-Size 45/90 or other speciality ruler.

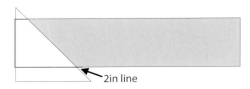

2in line

2 Sew along the diagonals to form eight half-square triangle units. Trim all dog ears and press open with the seams pressed towards the darker fabric.

make 8

3 Repeat with the other colour B 14in rectangle and the colour C 14in rectangle to make another eight half-square triangle units.

make 8

MAKING THE FLYING GEESE UNITS

4 Take two colour B 2½in squares and a colour A 2½in x 4½in rectangle and following the Important Techniques section make a flying geese unit. Repeat to make four units.

make 4

PIECING THE BLOCK

5 Sew the units together into rows as shown in the diagram below and then sew the rows together, pinning at every seam intersection to ensure a perfect match.

6 Piece the squares in rows 3 and 4 before sewing the flying geese units to either end. Press rows in alternate directions when possible so seams nest together nicely.

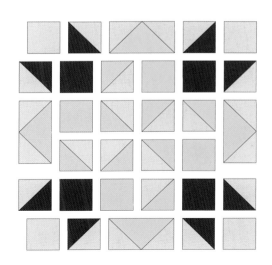

MAKING BLOCK 2 – ROCKY ROAD

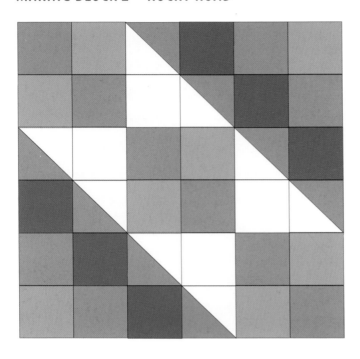

TOTAL STRIPS = 3
- ½ colour A medium strip (blue).
- 1 colour B medium strip (pink).
- ½ colour C dark strip (brown).
- 1 colour D light strip (cream).

CUTTING INSTRUCTIONS
- Colour A – cut eight 2½in squares.
- Colour B – cut ten 2½in squares,
  cut one 2½in x 14in rectangle.
- Colour C – cut six 2½in squares.
- Colour D – cut four 2½in squares,
  cut one 2½in x 14in rectangle.

MAKING THE HALF-SQUARE TRIANGLE UNITS

1 Take a colour B 14in rectangle and a colour D 14in rectangle and, referring to Important Techniques, cut eight sets of triangles using the Multi-Size 45/90 or other speciality ruler.

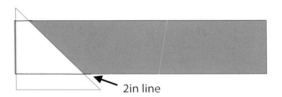

2in line

2 Sew along the diagonals to form eight half-square triangle units. Trim all dog ears and press open with the seams pressed towards the darker fabric.

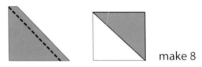

make 8

PIECING THE BLOCK

3 Sew the units together into rows as shown, right, and then sew the rows together, pinning at every seam intersection to ensure a perfect match. Press rows in alternate directions wherever possible so the seams nest together.

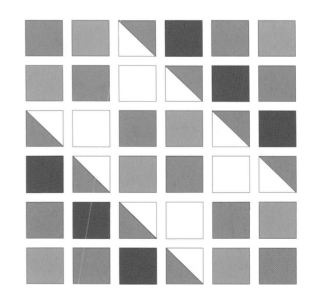

MAKING BLOCK 3 – STAR CHOICE

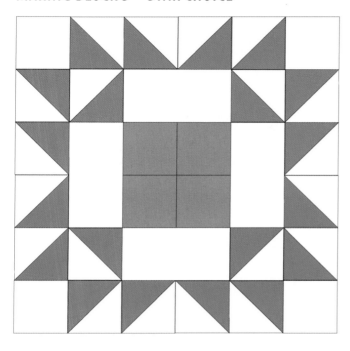

TOTAL STRIPS = 3½

- 2 colour A light strips (cream).
- 1 colour B dark strip (green).
- ½ colour C medium strip (brown).

CUTTING INSTRUCTIONS

- Colour A – cut one strip into:
  four 2½in squares,
  four rectangles 2½in x 4½in.
  Leave the other colour A strip and colour B strip uncut.
- Colour C – cut four 2½in squares.

MAKING THE HALF-SQUARE TRIANGLE UNITS

1 Take a colour A strip and the colour B strip and, referring to Important Techniques, cut twenty half-square triangle units using the Multi-Size 45/90 or other speciality ruler.

2in line

2 Trim all dog ears and press open with the seams pressed towards the darker fabric.

make 20

MAKING THE CENTRE

3 Sew four colour B squares together to form the centre of the block.

PIECING THE BLOCK

4 Sew the units together into rows as shown and then sew the rows together, pinning at every seam intersection to ensure a perfect match.

5 When sewing rows 3 and 4, sew the half-square triangles at the end of each row together first and then sew these to the rectangles. Press rows in alternate directions wherever possible so the seams nest together nicely.

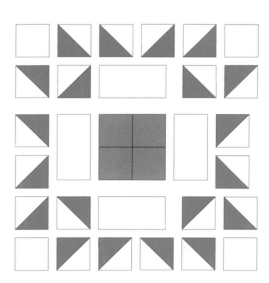

MAKING BLOCK 4 – ROLLING STONE

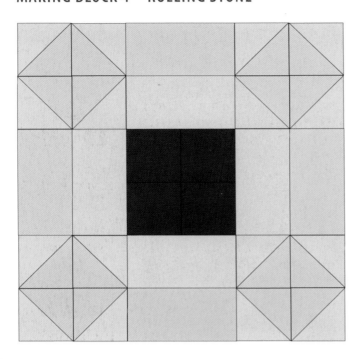

TOTAL STRIPS = 3½
- 1½ colour A medium strips (pink)
- 1½ colour B medium strips (blue)
- ½ colour C dark strip (brown)

CUTTING INSTRUCTIONS
- Colour C – from the half strip cut four 2½in squares.
- Leave the other strips uncut.

MAKING THE RAIL FENCE UNIT

1 Sew the colour A half strip to the colour B half strip and press towards the darker fabric.

2 Take your joined strips, trim the selvedge and cut into four 4½in squares.

MAKING THE HALF-SQUARE TRIANGLE UNITS

3 Take the colour A strip and the colour B strip and, referring to Important Techniques, cut sixteen sets of triangles using the Multi-Size 45/90 ruler or other speciality ruler.

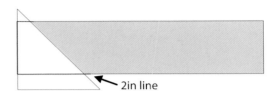

4 Sew along the diagonals to form sixteen half-square triangle units. Trim all dog ears. Press half with the seams pressed towards the darker fabric and the other half with the seams pressed towards the lighter fabric. This will allow the seams to nest together neatly when sewn together.

make 16

PIECING THE BLOCK

5 Sew the units together as shown and then sew the rows together, pinning at every seam intersection to ensure a perfect match. Press rows in alternate directions wherever possible so the seams nest together nicely.

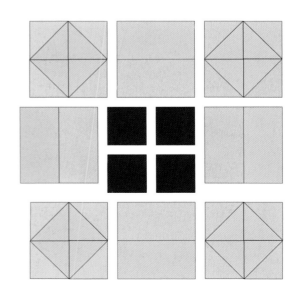

MAKING BLOCK 5 – ROLLING PINWHEEL

TOTAL STRIPS = 3½

- 2 colour A light strips (cream).
- 1 colour B dark strip (brown).
- ½ colour C medium strip (pink).

CUTTING INSTRUCTIONS

- Colour A – from one strip cut four rectangles 2½in x 8½in, from one strip cut sixteen 2½in squares.
- Colour B – cut four rectangles 2½in x 4½in, eight 2½in squares.
- Colour C – cut four rectangles 2½in x 4½in.

MAKING THE FLYING GEESE UNITS

1 Take two colour A 2½in squares and a colour C 2½in x 4½in rectangle and following Important Techniques make a flying geese unit. Repeat to make four of these units.

make 4

2 Using the same technique make a colour A square flip-over corner on the left side of a colour B 2½in x 4½in rectangle. Make four of these units.

make 4

3 Sew these two units together as shown in the diagram to create four of these units.

4 Take two colour B 2½in squares and a colour A 2½in x 8½in rectangle and using the same technique make four of these units.

make 4

5 Sew a colour A square to each end of two of these units. Press as shown in the diagram.

PIECING THE BLOCK

6 Sew the four central units together as shown. Sew the side units. Sew on the top units, pinning at every seam intersection to ensure a perfect match.

MAKING BLOCK 6 – UNION SQUARE

TOTAL STRIPS = 3½
- 1½ colour A medium strips (green).
- 1 colour B medium strips (pink).
- 1 colour C light strip (cream).

CUTTING INSTRUCTIONS
- Colour A – from the full strip cut four 2½in squares: the remainder of this strip will be used for the quarter-square triangles,
  – from the half strip cut one 2½in x 14in rectangle.
- Colour B – leave uncut.
- Colour C – cut eight 2½in squares,
  – cut one 2½in x 14in rectangle.

MAKING THE HALF-SQUARE TRIANGLE UNITS

1 Take the colour A 14in rectangle and the colour C 14in rectangle and referring to Important Techniques, cut eight sets of triangles using the Multi-Size 45/90 or other speciality ruler.

2in line

2 Sew along the diagonals to form eight half-square triangle units. Trim all dog ears and press open with seams pressed towards the darker fabric.

make 8

3 Sew a colour C square to the left of one unit as shown. Press towards the colour C square.

4 Sew a colour A square to the right of one unit as shown. Press to the colour A square.

5 Sew these two units together pinning at the seam intersection to ensure a perfect match. Repeat to make four of these units.

make 4

MAKING THE QUARTER-SQUARE TRIANGLE UNITS

6 Take the balance of the colour A strip and using the Multi-Size 45/90 as described in Important Techniques cut eight 4in quarter-square triangles.

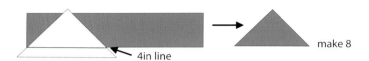

4in line

make 8

7 Repeat with the colour B strip to create eight colour B 4in quarter-square triangles.

make 8

8 Sew one colour A triangle to a colour B triangle as shown. Repeat to create eight of these units. Press to the darker colour. Trim any dog ears.

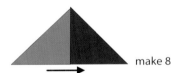

make 8

9 Take two of these units and sew together as shown, pinning at the seam intersection to ensure a perfect match. Repeat to create four quarter-square triangle units.

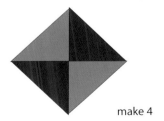

make 4

PIECING THE BLOCK

10 Join the units together as shown and then sew the rows together, pinning at every seam intersection to ensure a perfect match.

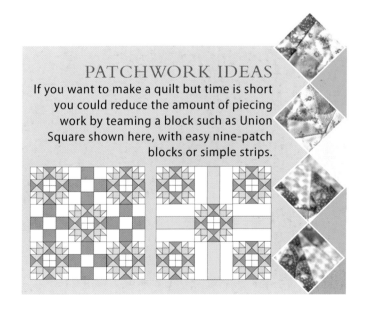

PATCHWORK IDEAS
If you want to make a quilt but time is short you could reduce the amount of piecing work by teaming a block such as Union Square shown here, with easy nine-patch blocks or simple strips.

MAKING BLOCK 7 – SPIRAL

TOTAL STRIPS = 4½

- 1½ colour A light strips (grey).
- 1½ colour B medium strips (pink).
- 1 colour C dark strip (brown).
- ½ colour D medium strip (blue).

CUTTING INSTRUCTIONS

- Colour A – from a full strip cut one rectangle 2½in x 27in,
  cut one rectangle 2½in x 8in
  – from half a strip cut one rectangle 2½in x 8in,
  cut four 2½in squares.
- Colour B – from a full strip cut one rectangle 2½in x 27in,
  – from half a strip cut eight 2½in squares.
- Colour C – cut one rectangle 2½in x 8in,
  cut four rectangles 2½in x 4½in.
- Colour D – cut one rectangle 2½in x 8in.

MAKING THE HALF-SQUARE TRIANGLE UNITS

1 Take a colour A 27in rectangle and a colour B 27in rectangle and, referring to Important Techniques, cut sixteen sets of triangles using the Multi-Size 45/90 or other speciality ruler.

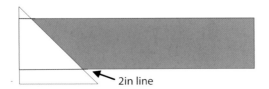

2in line

2 Sew along the diagonals to form sixteen half-square triangle units. Trim all dog ears and press open with seams pressed towards the darker fabric.

make 16

3 Repeat with the colour A 8in rectangle cut from the full strip and a colour C 8in rectangle to make four half-square triangle units.

make 4

4 Repeat with the colour A 8in rectangle cut from the half strip and colour D 8in rectangle to make four half-square triangle units.

make 4

MAKING THE FLYING GEESE UNITS

5 Take two colour B 2½in squares and a colour C 2½in x 4½in rectangle and following Important Techniques make a flying geese unit. Repeat to make four units.

make 4

PIECING THE BLOCK

6 Sew the units together into rows as shown and then sew the rows together, pinning at every seam intersection to ensure a perfect match. Piece the squares in rows 3 and 4 before sewing the flying geese units to either end. Press rows in alternate directions when possible so seams nest together nicely.

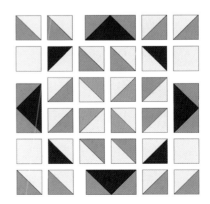

MAKING BLOCK 8 – GARDEN TRAIL

TOTAL STRIPS = 4
- 2 colour A medium strips (gold).
- 1½ colour B medium strips (green).
- ½ colour C dark strip (brown).

CUTTING INSTRUCTIONS
- Colour A – from one strip cut eight 2½in x 4½in rectangles, from the other strip cut twelve 2½in squares.
- Colour B – from the half strip cut four 2½in x 4½in rectangles, from the full strip cut ten 2½in squares.
- Colour C – cut six 2½in squares.

MAKING THE FLYING GEESE UNITS

1 Take two colour B 2½in squares and a colour A 2½in x 4½in rectangle and following Important Techniques make a flying geese unit. Repeat to make four of these units.

make 4

2 Repeat the above with colour A squares sewn on to colour B rectangles. Make four of these units.

make 4

PIECING THE BLOCK

3 Sew the units together as shown below and then sew the rows together, pinning at every seam intersection to ensure a perfect match. Piece the centre squares in rows 3 and 4 before sewing the flying geese units to either end. Press rows in alternate directions wherever possible so the seams nest together nicely.

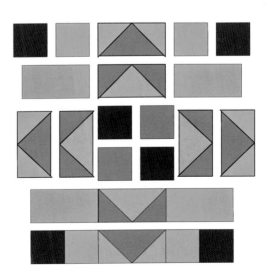

MAKING BLOCK 9 – CARD TRICK

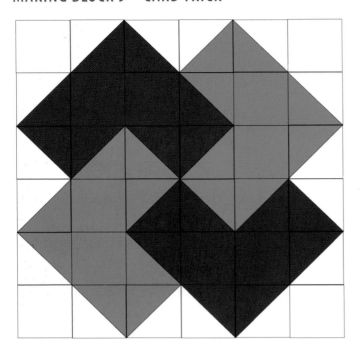

TOTAL STRIPS = 3
- 1 colour A dark strip (brown).
- 1 colour B medium strip (green).
- 1 colour C light strip (cream).

CUTTING INSTRUCTIONS
- Colour A – cut two 2½in x 14in rectangles, cut four 2½in squares.
- Colour B – cut two 2½in x 14in rectangles, cut four 2½in squares.
- Colour C – cut two 2½in x 14in rectangles, cut four 2½in squares.

MAKING THE HALF-SQUARE TRIANGLE UNITS

1 Take a colour A 14in rectangle and a colour B 14in rectangle and, referring to Important Techniques, cut eight sets of triangles using the Multi-Size 45/90 or other speciality ruler.

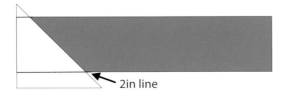

2in line

2 Sew along the diagonals to form eight half-square triangle units. Trim all dog ears and press open with seams pressed towards the darker fabric.

make 8

3 Repeat with a colour A and colour C rectangle to create eight half-square triangle units.

make 8

4 Repeat with a colour B and colour C rectangle to create eight half-square triangle units.

make 8

PIECING THE BLOCK

5 Sew the units together into rows as shown below and then sew the rows together, pinning at every seam intersection to ensure a perfect match. Be prepared to re-press some seams so they are pressed in opposite directions as they will then nest together more smoothly.

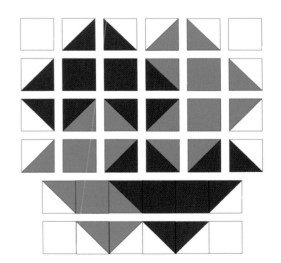

MAKING BLOCK 10 – MAPLE STAR

TOTAL STRIPS = 3
- 1½ colour A medium strips (blue).
- ½ colour B medium strip (gold).
- 1 colour C dark strip (brown).

CUTTING INSTRUCTIONS
- Colour A – from the full strip cut eight rectangles each 2½in x 4½in,
  – from the half strip cut eight 2½in squares.
- Colour B – cut four rectangles 2½in x 4½in.
- Colour C – cut twelve 2½in squares.

MAKING THE FLYING GEESE UNIT

1 Take two colour C 2½in squares and a colour A 2½in x 4½in rectangle and following Important Techniques make a flying geese unit. Repeat to make four units.

make 4

2 Sew a colour C rectangle to the bottom of each of the flying geese units. Press towards the rectangle.

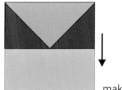

make 4

3 Sew a colour A square to a colour B square. Repeat to make four of these units. Press towards the dark fabric.

make 4

4 Sew a colour A rectangle to the top of these units, ensuring two are sewn with the dark square on the right and the other two are sewn with the dark square on the left. Press towards the rectangle.

5 Sew four colour A squares together to form the centre of the block.

PIECING THE BLOCK

6 Sew the units together as shown and then sew the rows together, pinning at every seam intersection to ensure a perfect match. Press rows in alternate directions wherever possible so the seams nest together nicely.

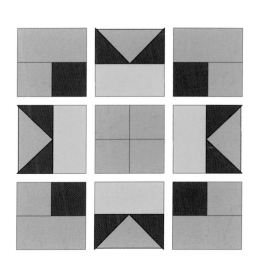

MAKING BLOCK 11 – ARROWHEAD

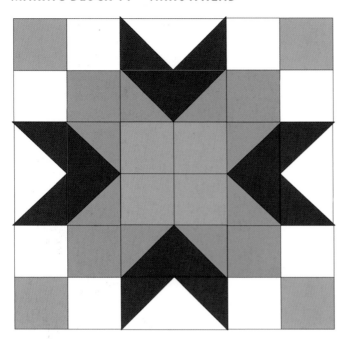

TOTAL STRIPS = 3½
- 1 colour A medium strip (pink).
- ½ colour B medium strip (blue).
- 1 colour C light strip (cream).
- 1 colour D dark strip (brown).

CUTTING INSTRUCTIONS
- Colour A – cut twelve 2½in squares.
- Colour B – cut eight 2½in squares.
- Colour C – cut eight 2½in squares, cut four rectangles 2½in x 4½in.
- Colour D – cut eight 2½in squares, cut four rectangles 2½in x 4½in.

MAKING THE FLYING GEESE UNITS

1 Take two colour D 2½in squares and a colour C 2½in x 4½in rectangle and following Important Techniques make a flying geese unit. Repeat to make four.

make 4

2 Repeat with colour A squares and colour D rectangles to make four flying geese units.

make 4

3 Sew these two flying geese units together. Press in the direction shown.

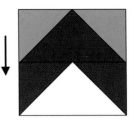

MAKING THE FOUR-PATCH UNITS

4 Sew a colour B square to a colour C square. Repeat to make four of these units. Press towards the dark fabric.

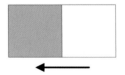

5 Sew a colour C square to a colour A square. Repeat to make four of these units. Press to the darker fabric.

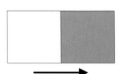

6 Sew the units together pinning at seam intersections to make four four-patch units.

make 4

PIECING THE BLOCKS

7 Sew four colour B squares together to form the centre of the block. Sew the units together as shown below and then sew the rows together, pinning at every seam intersection to ensure a perfect match. Press rows in alternate directions when possible so seams nest together nicely.

MAKING BLOCK 12 – STREAK OF LIGHTNING

TOTAL STRIPS = 2½

- ½ colour A medium strip (brown).
- ½ colour B medium strip (pink).
- ½ colour C medium strip (green).
- ½ colour D light strip (cream).
- ½ colour E medium strip (blue).

CUTTING INSTRUCTIONS

- From each half strip cut eight 2½in squares. You will have four squares spare.
- Note: we have given the instructions as though you had five half strips left. You will only have three so this is where you use up the offcuts from the other blocks.

PIECING THE BLOCK

Lay out the squares in the pattern shown. Sew the squares together into rows and then sew the rows together, pinning at every seam intersection to ensure a perfect match. Press rows in alternate directions wherever possible so the seams nest together nicely.

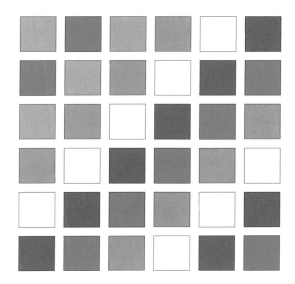

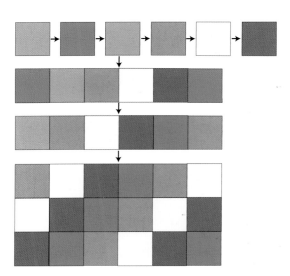

ASSEMBLING THE QUILT

SEWING THE BLOCKS TOGETHER

1 Once all the blocks are complete cut twenty 2½in squares for the sashing squares from the offcuts.

2 Lay out your blocks with the sashing and sashing squares and when you are happy with the effect sew the sashing rows together as shown. You need five rows. Press towards the sashing strips.

3 Sew the blocks together with sashing strips on both sides of the first block in a row and on the right of the other two blocks. Press towards the sashing strips.

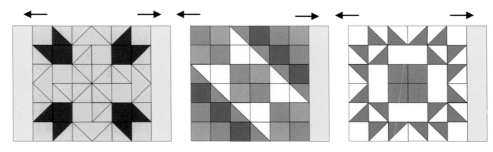

4 Sew the rows together pinning at every seam intersection to ensure a perfect match. Press the quilt top.

ADDING THE BORDER

5 Join the 4½in border strips into one continuous length. Determine the vertical measurement from top to bottom of the quilt top and cut two lengths to this measurement (see Adding Borders). Sew these to either side of the quilt, pinning and easing where necessary.

6 Determine the horizontal measurement from side to side through the centre of the quilt top. Cut two lengths to this measurement and sew to the top and bottom of the quilt, pinning and easing where necessary.

7 Your quilt top is now complete. Quilt as desired and bind to finish – see Quilting and Binding a Quilt.

Nicky's variation of our Classic Sampler is in a spring-like range from April Cornell for Moda called Nature's Chorus. The Jelly Roll™ is a mixture of pale blues and yellows and makes for an extremely gentle quilt which would enhance the look of any room. The quilt was longarm quilted by The Quilt Room.

BIG AND BOLD
SAMPLER QUILT

This stunning quilt is made up of five 16in blocks linked together with an easy connector block. In this big and bold design we have used eye-catching Kaffe Fassett fabrics, together with a solid purple, which we think is a perfect combination.

Each of the blocks in this quilt would look great used in different ways. For example, Japanese Star would be the perfect centre for a medallion quilt, while we can imagine Chequered Star and Carpenter's Wheel alternating with other blocks to create gorgeous quilts. If you want to make a quilt from just one repeated block then Blackford Beauty or Railroad Crossing would be ideal – see our Peppermint Whirls Quilt in the Pick 'n' Mix section, which features the Blackford Beauty block. Think big and bold and endless possibilities lie before you!

The variation quilt at the end of this chapter shows that the design looks equally as good in a more subtle colour scheme, using reproduction fabrics.

BIG AND BOLD SAMPLER QUILT

VITAL STATISTICS

QUILT SIZE	60in x 60in
BLOCK SIZE	16in
BLOCKS PER QUILT	5 sampler blocks and 4 connector blocks
SETTING	3 x 3 + 6in wide border

REQUIREMENTS

- One Jelly Roll™
- 2yd (2m) of background and border fabric
- Binding made from Jelly Roll™ strips
- Multi-Size 45/90 ruler or other speciality tool for making half-square and quarter-square triangles

SORTING YOUR JELLY ROLL STRIPS

- Sort your strips before you start your quilt. Each block gives its own strip requirements but it is important to sort them before you start and label the strips once sorted. Be prepared to play around with them until you are happy with the results. Don't be afraid to adjust or revise your choices as the blocks emerge.
- *Important*: when you need more than one strip for a colour, i.e., three strips for colour A in the Railroad Crossing block, make sure they look similar. You don't want two strips of yellow and one strip of a pink. Select three strips of a similar colour.
- The Cutting Chart below gives the strips required for each block and will help you sort the strips.

CUTTING INSTRUCTIONS

Background and border fabric:

- Cut twelve 2½in wide strips across the width of the fabric and set aside for the connector blocks.
- Cut six 6½in wide strips across the width of the fabric and set aside for the borders.

CUTTING CHART FOR THE BIG AND BOLD SAMPLER QUILT

BLOCK	COLOUR A STRIPS	COLOUR B STRIPS	COLOUR C STRIPS	COLOUR D STRIPS	COLOUR E STRIPS	TOTAL STRIPS
1 Railroad Crossing	3	1	2	½		**6½**
2 Carpenter's Wheel	3	1	2			**6**
3 Japanese Star	2½	2	1	1		**6½**
4 Chequered Star	2	1	1	1	½	**5½**
5 Blackford Beauty	1½	1½	1	1	½	**5½**
6 Connector Block	1	1	1	1		**4**
Binding						**6**
					TOTAL STRIPS	**40**

MAKING BLOCK 1 – RAILROAD CROSSING

TOTAL STRIPS = 6½
- 3 strips colour A (yellow).
- 1 strip colour B (red).
- 2 strips colour C (blue).
- ½ strip colour D (brown).

CUTTING INSTRUCTIONS
- Colour A – from one strip cut eight 2½in squares and four 2½in x 4½in rectangles. Leave the remaining one and a half strips for half-square and quarter-square triangle units.
- Colour B – cut twelve 2½in squares.
- Colour C – from one strip cut four 2½in squares. Leave the remaining three-quarter strip for quarter-square triangles and the remaining full strip for half-square triangle units.
- Colour D – cut eight 2½in squares.

MAKING THE HALF-SQUARE TRIANGLE UNITS

1 Take a colour A full strip and colour C full strip and referring to Important Techniques cut sixteen sets of triangles using the Multi-Size 45/90 or other ruler.

2 Sew along the diagonals to form sixteen half-square triangle units. Trim dog ears and press seams towards the darker fabric.

  make 16

MAKING THE QUARTER-SQUARE TRIANGLE UNITS

3 Take a colour A full strip and using the Multi-Size 45/90 and cut eight 4in quarter-square triangles as in Important Techniques. Repeat with the colour C three-quarter strip to create eight colour C 4in quarter-square triangles.

 make 8  make 8

4 Sew one colour A triangle to a colour C triangle. Repeat to create eight units. Press to the darker colour. Trim any dog ears.

5 Take two of these units and sew together, pinning at the seam intersection to ensure a perfect match. Repeat to create four quarter-square triangle units.

MAKING THE FLYING GEESE UNITS

6 Take two colour D 2½in squares and a Colour A 2½in x 4½in rectangle and following Important Techniques make a flying geese unit. Repeat to make four of these units.

 make 4

PIECING THE BLOCK

7 Sew the quarter-square triangle units to the flying geese units and press as shown. Sew the nine patch corner units together and press as shown. Sew the four centre squares together. Join the units together and then sew the rows together, pinning at every seam intersection. Press rows in alternate directions when possible so seams nest together.

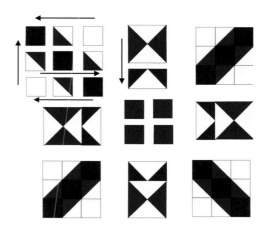

MAKING BLOCK 2 – CARPENTER'S WHEEL

TOTAL STRIPS = 6
- 3 strips colour A (red).
- 1 strip colour B (purple).
- 2 strips colour C (aqua).

CUTTING INSTRUCTIONS
- Colour A – from one strip cut eight 2½in x 4½in rectangles. – from one strip cut eight 2½in squares. Leave the remaining one and a half strips for half-square triangle units.
- Colour B – cut the strip into two halves.
- Colour C – from one strip cut eight 2½in squares. Leave the remaining one and a half strips for half-square triangle units.

MAKING THE HALF-SQUARE TRIANGLE UNITS

1 Take the colour A full strip and the colour C full strip and, referring to Important Techniques, cut sixteen sets of triangles using the Multi-Size 45/90 or other speciality ruler.

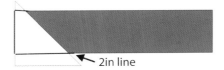

2in line

2 Sew along the diagonals to form sixteen half-square triangle units. Trim all dog ears and press open with the seams pressed towards the darker fabric.

  Make 16

3 Repeat with the colour A half strip and one of the colour B half strips to make another twelve half-square triangle units.

Make 12

4 Repeat with the colour C half strip and the other colour B half strip to make another twelve half-square triangle units.

Make 12

MAKING THE FLYING GEESE UNITS

5 Take two colour C 2½in squares and a Colour A 2½in x 4½in rectangle and following Important Techniques make a flying geese unit. Repeat to make four units.

Make 4

PIECING THE BLOCK

6 Following the diagram below, sew the corner units together, pressing as shown and pinning at every seam intersection to ensure a perfect match.

7 Sew two half-square triangle units together as shown and sew to one side of the colour A rectangle. Sew the flying geese unit to the other side. Press as shown.

8 Sew the centre squares together. Join the units together and then sew the rows together, pinning at every seam intersection to ensure a perfect match. Press rows in alternate directions wherever possible so seams nest together nicely.

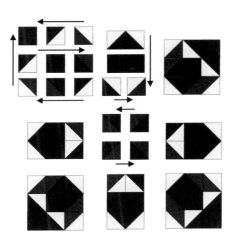

MAKING BLOCK 3 – JAPANESE STAR

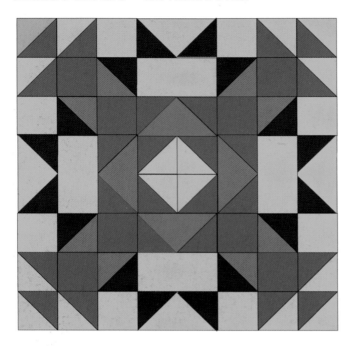

TOTAL STRIPS = 6½
- 2½ strips colour A (pink).
- 2 strips colour B (blue).
- 1 strip colour C (orange).
- 1 strip colour D (brown).

CUTTING INSTRUCTIONS
- Colour A – from one strip cut eight 2½in x 4½in rectangles.
  – from the half strip cut eight 2½in squares and leave the remaining strip for half-square triangle units.
- Colour B – from one strip cut sixteen 2½in squares and leave the remaining strip for half-square triangle units.
- Colour C – cut four 2½in x 4½in rectangles and leave the remaining half strip for half-square triangles.
- Colour D – cut eight 2½in squares and leave the remaining half strip for half-square triangles.

MAKING THE HALF-SQUARE TRIANGLE UNITS
1 Take a colour A strip and a colour B strip and, referring to Important Techniques, cut sixteen sets of triangles using the Multi-Size 45/90 or other speciality ruler.

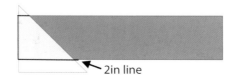

2in line

2 Sew along the diagonals to form sixteen half-square triangle units. Trim all dog ears and press open with seams pressed towards the darker fabric.

  Make 16

3 Repeat with the colour C half strip and the colour D half strip to make another eight half-square triangle units.

 Make 8

MAKING THE FLYING GEESE UNITS
4 Take two colour D 2½in squares and a Colour A 2½in x 4½in rectangle and following Important Techniques make a flying geese unit. Repeat to make four units.

 Make 4

5 Repeat the previous step with colour B squares sewn on to colour C rectangles. Make four of these units.

 Make 4

PIECING THE BLOCK
6 Sew the nine-patch corner units together and press as shown in the diagram below. Sew the flying geese units to each side of a colour A rectangle and press as shown. Sew the four centre squares together.

7 Join the units together and then sew the rows together, pinning at seam intersections to ensure a perfect match. Press rows in alternate directions when possible so seams nest together nicely.

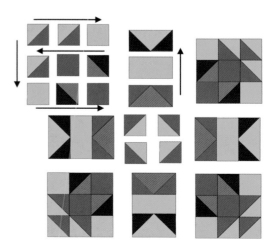

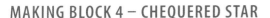

MAKING BLOCK 4 – CHEQUERED STAR

TOTAL STRIPS = 5½

- 2 strips colour A (green).
- 1 strip colour B (brown).
- 1 strip colour C (pink).
- 1 strip colour D (black).
- ½ strip colour E (purple).

CUTTING INSTRUCTIONS

- Colour A – cut twenty-eight 2½in squares.
- Colour B – cut four 2½in squares and four 2½in x 4½in rectangles.
- Colour C – cut four 2½in squares and leave the rest for quarter-square triangles.
- Colour D – cut four 2½in squares and leave the rest for quarter-square triangles.
- Colour E – cut eight 2½in squares.

MAKING THE FLYING GEESE UNITS

1 Take two colour A 2½in squares and a Colour B 2½in x 4½in rectangle and following Important Techniques make a flying geese unit. Repeat to make four units.

Make 4

MAKING THE QUARTER-SQUARE TRIANGLE UNITS

2 Take the colour C strip and using the Multi-Size 45/90 as described in Important Techniques cut eight 4in quarter-square triangles.

Make 8

3 Repeat with the colour D strip to create eight colour D 4in quarter-square triangles.

Make 8

4 Sew one colour C triangle to a colour D triangle as shown. Repeat to create eight of these units. Press to the darker colour. Trim any dog ears.

Make 8

5 Take two of these units and sew together as shown, pinning at the seam intersection to ensure a perfect match. Repeat to create four quarter-square triangle units.

Make 8

PIECING THE BLOCK

6 Sew the nine-patch corner units together and press as shown below. Sew the quarter-square triangle units to the flying geese unit and press as shown. Sew the four centre squares together.

7 Join the units together and then sew the rows together, pinning at every seam intersection to ensure a perfect match. Press rows in alternate directions wherever possible so the seams nest together nicely.

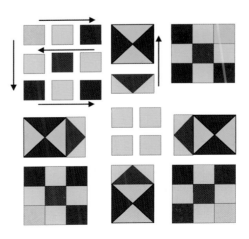

MAKING BLOCK 5 – BLACKFORD BEAUTY

TOTAL STRIPS = 5½
- 1½ colour A strips (orange).
- 1½ colour B strips (lime).
- 1 colour C strip (blue).
- 1 colour D strip (aqua).
- ½ colour E strip (brown).

CUTTING INSTRUCTIONS
- Colour A – cut twenty 2½in squares.
- Colour B – cut eight 2½in x 6½in rectangles.
- Colour C – cut sixteen 2½in squares.
- Colour D – cut twelve 2½in squares.
- Colour E – cut eight 2½in squares.

MAKING THE FLIP-OVER CORNER UNITS

1 Take two colour C 2½in squares and a colour B 2½in x 6½in rectangle and following Important Techniques on making flying geese units, sew one square to the bottom left and the other square to the top right of the rectangle to form unit A. Repeat to make four of these units.

A   Make 4

2 Repeat the step above, sewing a colour C 2½in square to the top left and one to the bottom right of the colour B 2½in x 6½in rectangle to form unit B. Repeat to make four of these units.

B   Make 4

PIECING THE BLOCK

3 Sew a unit A to a unit B as shown below and repeat to make four. Sew the four centre squares together. Sew the four nine-patch corner units together and press as shown.

4 Join the units together and then sew the rows together, pinning at every seam intersection to ensure a perfect match. Press rows in alternate directions wherever possible so the seams nest together nicely.

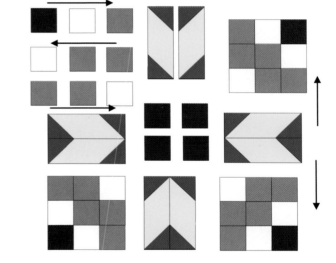

MAKING THE CONNECTOR BLOCK

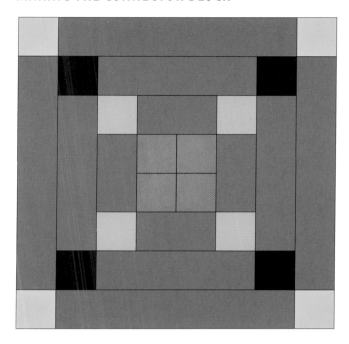

CUTTING INSTRUCTIONS

- Take the four Jelly Roll™ strips allocated for the connector blocks and cut each strip into sixteen 2½in squares to make a total of sixty-four.
- Take the twelve 2½in wide background strips allocated for the connector blocks and cut as follows:
  – take two strips and subcut each into eight rectangles 2½in x 4½in to make a total of sixteen rectangles,
  – take four strips and subcut each into four rectangles 2½in x 8½in to make a total of sixteen rectangles,
  – take six strips and subcut each into three rectangles 2½in x 12½in to make a total of sixteen rectangles. You will have two spare.

PIECING THE BLOCK

1 Sew four 2½in squares together to create the centre, pressing as shown and pinning at the centre seam to ensure a perfect match. We used squares of the same fabric but you could choose to make your connector blocks scrappier.

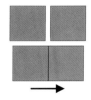

2 Take four 2½in x 4½in background rectangles and sew two to the sides of the centre. Press as shown. Sew a 2½in square to both sides of the other two rectangles and sew to the top and bottom of the centre unit. Press as shown.

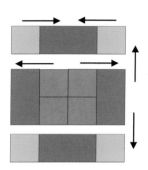

3 Repeat the step above but with four 2½in x 8½in background rectangles.

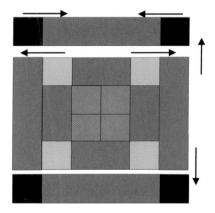

4 Repeat the step above but with four 2½in x 12½in background rectangles.

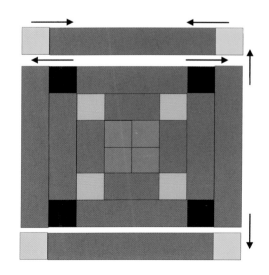

ASSEMBLING THE QUILT

SEWING YOUR BLOCKS TOGETHER

1 Referring to the diagram, right, sew the blocks together to form rows, alternating the connector blocks with the sampler blocks. If you always press towards the connector blocks your seams will nest together nicely. Pin at every seam intersection to ensure a perfect match.

ADDING THE BORDER

2 Join the 6½in border strips into one long length. Determine the vertical measurement from top to bottom of the quilt top (see Adding Borders). Cut two lengths to this measurement and sew to either side of the quilt, pinning and easing where necessary.

3 Determine the horizontal measurement from side to side through the centre of your quilt top. Cut two lengths to this measurement and sew to the top and bottom of the quilt, pinning and easing where necessary.

4 Your quilt top is now complete. Quilt as desired and bind to finish – see Quilting and Binding a Quilt. To create a scrappy binding, cut each binding strip into four quarters (approximately 2½in x 10½in). Sew the quarters into a continuous length, making sure you don't have similar fabrics next to each other.

Our Big and Bold variation quilt was made by Sarah Short, who is our 'Saturday Girl' at The Quilt Room. She used a reproduction civil war Jelly Roll™ and we loved her choice of background fabric, which looks perfect. The quilt was longarm quilted by The Quilt Room in a traditional feather design.

SNOWBALL
SAMPLER QUILT

This sunny sampler quilt uses a repeated snowball block to unify the design and these are used in an alternating layout with eighteen sampler blocks, all 8in square, in a bright colour scheme of pinks, blues, yellows, greens and creams. You could, of course, choose to sew the blocks together in many different ways but we rather liked connecting them together with the snowball block. Many of the blocks we have selected for this quilt are star blocks, which create a nice sense of movement.

As these are smaller blocks, and in order not to waste any fabric, we have often sorted our strips into quarters. The sorting instructions will tell you that you sometimes only need one quarter of a strip. As we always base our calculations on a strip being 42in long, the quarter strip measurement is therefore 10½in long, the half strip is 21in and the three-quarter strip is 31½in long.

SNOWBALL SAMPLER QUILT

VITAL STATISTICS

QUILT SIZE	48in x 64in
BLOCK SIZE	8in square
BLOCKS PER QUILT	18 sampler blocks and 17 snowball blocks
SETTING	35 blocks + 4in wide border

REQUIREMENTS

- One Jelly Roll™
- 1.25m (1¼yd) of background fabric
- 1.25m (1¼yd) of accent fabric for snowball corners and borders
- Spare Jelly Roll™ strips are used for the binding
- Multi-Size 45/90 or other speciality ruler for making half-square triangles

SORTING YOUR JELLY ROLL STRIPS

- Sort your strips before you start your quilt. Each block gives its own strip requirements and it is important to sort them before you start your quilt and then label the strips once sorted. You can change anything around and place your lights and darks in different places depending on the strips chosen, so be prepared to play around with them until you are happy with the results. Our cutting chart opposite gives the strips required for each block and will help you to sort the strips. You have plenty to play with as you only need twenty-nine and a half for the blocks.
- Six strips are needed for the binding but don't allocate these until all your choices for the blocks have been made. You will have four and a half strips spare.

CUTTING INSTRUCTIONS

Background fabric:
- Cut five 8½in wide strips across the width of the fabric.
- Subcut each of these strip into four 8½in squares. You need seventeen – three are spare.

Accent fabric:
- Cut ten 4½in wide strips across the width of the fabric.
- Set six aside for the borders.
- Subcut each of the remaining four strips into nine 4½in squares for the snowball corners. You need thirty-six.

MAKING THE SNOWBALL BLOCKS

There are seventeen snowball blocks in total in this quilt – eight have a single corner unit, four have two corner units and five have units at each corner.

1   Mark a diagonal line from corner to corner on the wrong side of the 4½in square snowball corners. This can be done with a pencil or a speedier alternative is to make a fold across the diagonal.

2   With right sides together, lay a marked square on one corner of an 8½in background square, aligning the outer edges. Sew across the diagonal, using the marked diagonal line as the stitching line.

3   Flip the square over and press towards the outside of the block. Trim the excess fabric from the snowball corner but do not trim the background fabric. Although this creates a little more bulk, the background fabric helps keep your patchwork in shape. Make seventeen of these units and set eight aside to remain with only one snowball corner.

make 8

4   Take four of the remaining units and sew another snowball corner as shown. Press to the background fabric.

make 4

5   Take the remaining five units and sew a snowball corner to each corner as shown. Press to the background fabric.

make 5

CUTTING CHART FOR THE SNOWBALL SAMPLER QUILT

BLOCK NUMBER	COLOUR A	COLOUR B	COLOUR C	COLOUR D	COLOUR E	TOTAL STRIPS
1 Eccentric Star	1	¼	½			1¾
2 Windblown Square	1	½	½			2
3 Spinning Star	1	½	½			2
4 Friendship Star	½	¾	¼			1½
5 King's Crown	½	¼	¼	½		1½
6 Buckeye Beauty	¾	½	¼			1½
7 Spinner	¼	¼	¼	½	¼	1½
8 Flying Dutchman	1	1				2
9 Fox and Geese	1	½	½			2
10 Sawtooth Star	¾	½	½			1¾
11 Fan	¾	¼	½			1½
12 Water Wheel	½	½	¼			1¼
13 X-Quartet	½	½	½			1½
14 Shaded Trail	¾	½	¼			1½
15 Nelson's Victory	½	¼	½			1¼
16 Geese in Flight	¾	¼	½			1½
17 Evening Star	¾	½	½			1¾
18 Martha Washington Star	1	¼	½			1¾
Binding						6
					TOTAL STRIPS	35½

MAKING BLOCK 1 – ECCENTRIC STAR

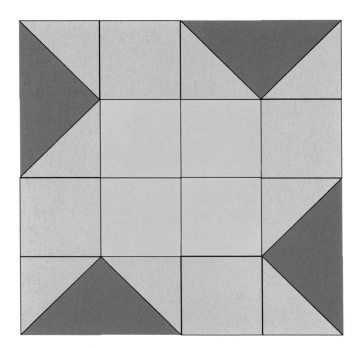

TOTAL STRIPS = 1¾
- 1 colour A strip (pink).
- ¼ colour B strip (yellow).
- ½ colour C strip (aqua).

CUTTING INSTRUCTIONS
- Colour A – cut twelve 2½in squares.
- Colour B – cut four 2½in squares.
- Colour C – cut four rectangles 2½in x 4½in.

MAKING THE FLYING GEESE UNITS

1 Take two colour A 2½in squares and a colour C 2½in x 4½in rectangle and following Important Techniques make a flying geese unit. Repeat to make four units.

 make 4

PIECING THE BLOCK

2 Sew a colour A square to a colour B square and then sew this to the flying geese unit. Press in the directions shown by the arrows on the diagram. Sew the units together, pinning at every seam intersection to ensure a perfect match.

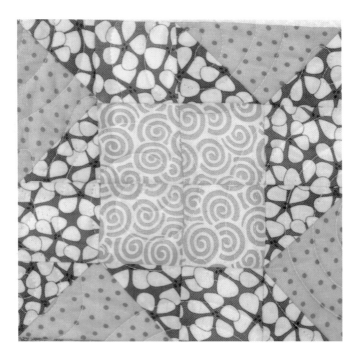

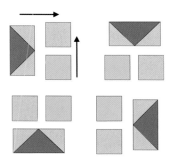

MAKING BLOCK 2 – WINDBLOWN SQUARE

TOTAL STRIPS = 2
- 1 colour A strip (white).
- ½ colour B strip (yellow).
- ½ colour C strip (blue).

CUTTING INSTRUCTIONS
- Colour A – cut sixteen 2½in squares.
- Colour B – cut four rectangles 2½in x 4½in.
- Colour C – cut four rectangles 2½in x 4½in.

MAKING THE FLYING GEESE UNITS

1 Take two colour A 2½in squares and a colour C 2½in x 4½in rectangle and following Important Techniques make a flying geese unit. Repeat to make four units.

 make 4

2 Take two colour A 2½in squares and a colour B 2½in x 4½in rectangle. Sew one square to the left-hand side of the rectangle and then sew the second square to the diagonal corner. Repeat to make four of these units.

 make 4

PIECING THE BLOCK

3 Sew the units together as shown, pinning at every seam intersection to ensure a perfect match.

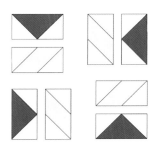

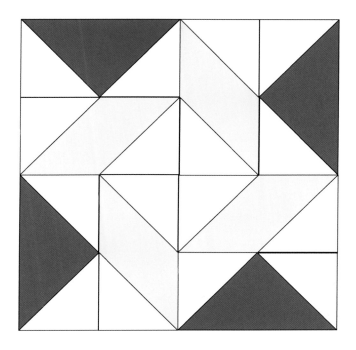

PATCHWORK IDEAS
The Windblown Square block makes an attractive design on its own, repeated in rows. You could also team it with alternate Snowball blocks for a different look.

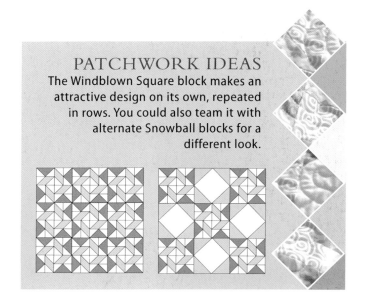

MAKING BLOCK 3 – SPINNING STAR

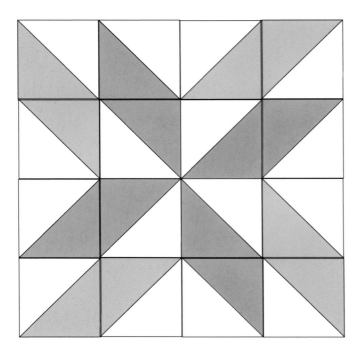

2 Sew along the diagonals to form eight half-square triangle units. Trim all dog ears and press open, with the seams pressed towards the darker fabric.

make 8

3 Repeat with the other colour A half strip and the colour C half strip to make another eight half-square triangle units.

make 8

TOTAL STRIPS = 2
- 1 colour A strip (white).
- ½ colour B strip (pink).
- ½ colour C strip (aqua).

CUTTING INSTRUCTIONS
- Colour A – cut into two separate half strips for half-square triangle units.

MAKING THE HALF-SQUARE TRIANGLE UNITS
1 Take a colour A half strip and a colour B half strip and referring to Important Techniques cut eight sets of triangles using the Multi-Size 45/90 ruler or other speciality ruler.

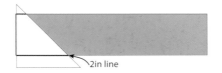

2in line

PIECING THE BLOCK
4 Sew the units together into rows, pinning at every seam intersection to ensure a perfect match. Press rows in alternate directions wherever possible so the seams nest together nicely.

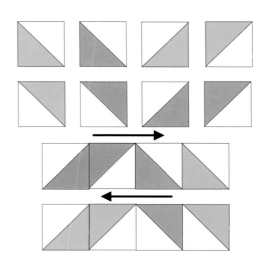

MAKING BLOCK 4 – FRIENDSHIP STAR

TOTAL STRIPS = 1½
- ½ colour A strip (blue).
- ¾ colour B strip (yellow).
- ¼ colour C strip (green).

CUTTING INSTRUCTIONS
- Colour A – cut into two separate quarter strips for half-square triangle units.
- Colour B – cut four rectangles 2½in x 4½in. Leave the remaining quarter strip for half-square triangle units.

MAKING THE HALF-SQUARE TRIANGLE UNITS

1 Take a colour A quarter strip and a colour B quarter strip and referring to Important Techniques cut four sets of triangles using the Multi-Size 45/90 or other speciality ruler.

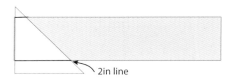

2in line

2 Sew along the diagonals to form four half-square triangle units. Trim all dog ears and press open, with the seams pressed towards the darker fabric.

make 4

3 Repeat with the other colour A quarter strip and the colour C quarter strip to make another four half-square triangle units.

make 4

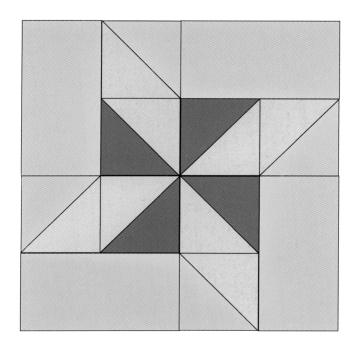

PIECING THE BLOCK

4 Join the half-square triangle units together. Sew them to the rectangles as shown in the diagram and press.

5 Sew the units together, pinning at every seam intersection to ensure a perfect match.

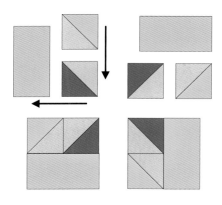

MAKING BLOCK 5 – KING'S CROWN

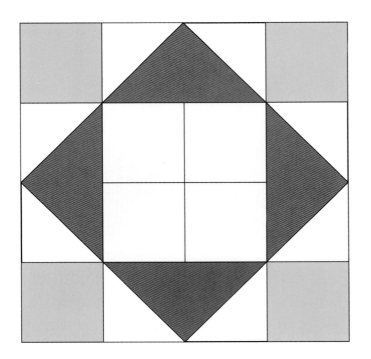

TOTAL STRIPS = 1½
- ½ colour A strip (white).
- ¼ colour B strip (yellow).
- ¼ colour C strip (green).
- ½ colour D strip (pink).

CUTTING INSTRUCTIONS
- Colour A – cut eight 2½in squares.
- Colour B – cut four 2½in squares.
- Colour C – cut four 2½in squares.
- Colour D – cut four rectangles 2½in x 4½in.

MAKING THE FLYING GEESE UNITS

1 Take two colour A 2½in squares and a colour D 2½in x 4½in rectangle and following Important Techniques make a flying geese unit. Repeat to make four of these units.

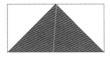 make 4

PIECING THE BLOCK

2 Join the units together as shown below and then sew the rows together, pinning at every seam intersection to ensure a perfect match.

3 Piece the centre squares in rows 2 and 3 before sewing the flying geese units to either end. Press rows in alternate directions wherever possible so the seams nest together nicely.

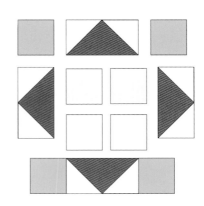

MAKING BLOCK 6 – BUCKEYE BEAUTY

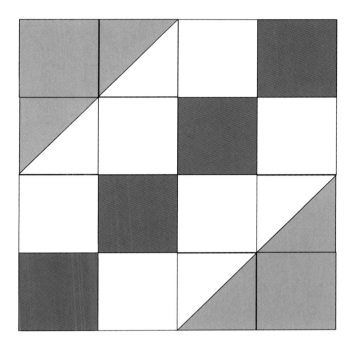

MAKING THE HALF-SQUARE TRIANGLE UNITS

1 Take a colour A quarter strip and a colour B quarter strip and referring to Important Techniques cut four sets of triangles using the Multi-Size 45/90 or other speciality ruler.

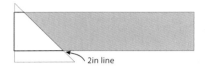

2 Sew along the diagonals to form four half-square triangle units. Trim all dog ears and press open, with the seams pressed towards the darker fabric.

make 4

TOTAL STRIPS = 1½

- ¾ colour A strip (white).
- ½ colour B strip (mauve).
- ¼ colour C strip (blue).

CUTTING INSTRUCTIONS

- Colour A – cut six 2½in squares. Leave the remaining quarter strip for half-square triangle units.
- Colour B – cut two 2½in squares. Leave the remaining quarter strip for half-square triangle units.
- Colour C – cut four 2½in squares.

PIECING THE BLOCK

3 Sew the units together into rows as shown, pinning at every seam intersection to ensure a perfect match. Press rows in alternate directions wherever possible so the seams nest together nicely.

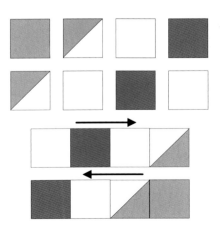

MAKING BLOCK 7 – SPINNER

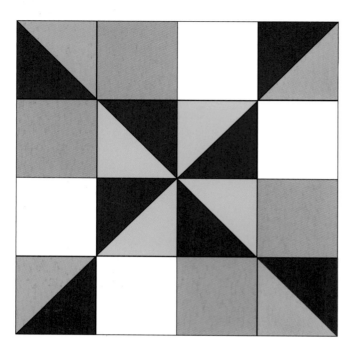

TOTAL STRIPS = 1½

- ¼ colour A strip (white).
- ¼ colour B strip (mauve).
- ¼ colour C strip (green).
- ½ colour D strip (purple).
- ¼ colour E strip (pink).

CUTTING INSTRUCTIONS

- Colour A – cut four 2½in squares.
- Colour B – cut four 2½in squares.
- Colour D – cut the half strip into two separate quarter strips to make half-square triangle units.

MAKING THE HALF-SQUARE TRIANGLE UNITS

1 Take a colour D quarter strip and a colour C quarter strip and referring to Important Techniques cut four sets of triangles using the Multi-Size 45/90 or other speciality ruler.

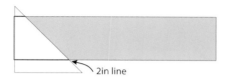

2 Sew along the diagonals to form four half-square triangle units. Trim all dog ears and press open, with the seams pressed towards the darker fabric.

3 Repeat with the other colour D quarter strip and the colour E quarter strip to make another four half-square triangle units.

PIECING THE BLOCK

4 Join the units together into rows as shown below and then sew the rows together, pinning at every seam intersection to ensure a perfect match. Press rows in alternate directions when possible so seams nest together nicely.

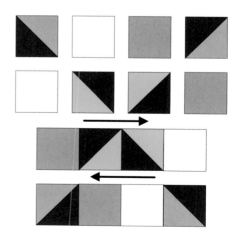

MAKING BLOCK 8 – FLYING DUTCHMAN

TOTAL STRIPS = 2
- 1 colour A strip (white).
- 1 colour B strip (mauve).

CUTTING INSTRUCTIONS
- Colour A – cut sixteen 2½in squares.
- Colour B – cut eight rectangles 2½in x 4½in.

MAKING THE FLYING GEESE UNITS
1 Take two colour A 2½in squares and a colour B 2½in x 4½in rectangle and following Important Techniques make a flying geese unit. Repeat to make eight of these units.

 make 8

PIECING THE BLOCK
2 Sew the flying geese units together as shown, pinning at every seam intersection to ensure a perfect match.

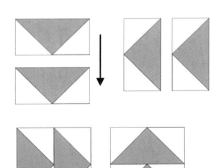

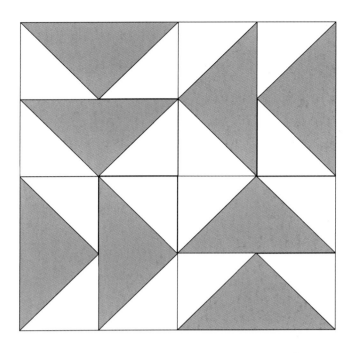

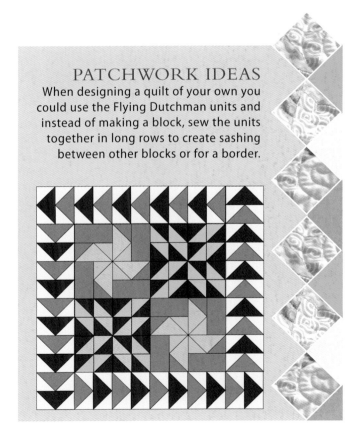

PATCHWORK IDEAS
When designing a quilt of your own you could use the Flying Dutchman units and instead of making a block, sew the units together in long rows to create sashing between other blocks or for a border.

MAKING BLOCK 9 – FOX AND GEESE

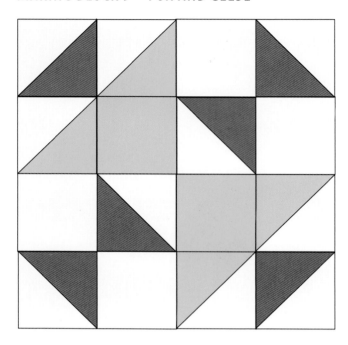

TOTAL STRIPS = 2

- 1 colour A strip (yellow).
- ½ colour B strip (green).
- ½ colour C strip (pink).

CUTTING INSTRUCTIONS:

- Colour A – cut the strip into one half strip and two separate quarter strips,
  set the half strip and one of the quarter strips aside for half-square triangle units,
  cut the remaining quarter strip into four 2½in squares.
- Colour B – cut two 2½in squares and keep the remainder of the half strip for half-square triangle units.

MAKING THE HALF-SQUARE TRIANGLE UNITS

1 Take a colour A quarter strip and a colour B quarter strip and referring to Important Techniques cut four sets of triangles using the Multi-Size 45/90 ruler or other speciality ruler.

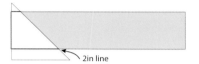

2 Sew along the diagonals to form four half-square triangle units. Trim all dog ears and press open, with the seams pressed towards the darker fabric.

make 4

3 Repeat with the colour A half strip and the colour C half strip to make six half-square triangle units.

make 6

PIECING THE BLOCK

4 Join the units together into rows as shown below and then sew the rows together, pinning at every seam intersection to ensure a perfect match. Press rows in alternate directions wherever possible so the seams nest together nicely.

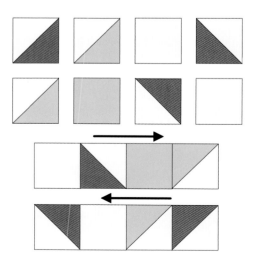

MAKING BLOCK 10 – SAWTOOTH STAR

TOTAL STRIPS = 1¾
- ¾ colour A strip (white).
- ½ colour B strip (yellow).
- ½ colour C strip (mauve).

CUTTING INSTRUCTIONS
- Colour A – from the three-quarter strip cut four rectangles 2½in x 4½in.
  Set the remaining quarter strip aside for half-square triangle units.
- Colour B – from the half strip cut four 2½in squares.
  Set the remaining quarter strip aside for half-square triangle units.
- Colour C – cut eight 2½in squares.

MAKING THE HALF-SQUARE TRIANGLE UNITS

1 Take a colour A quarter strip and a colour B quarter strip and referring to Important Techniques cut four sets of triangles using the Multi-Size 45/90 or other speciality ruler.

2 Sew along the diagonals to form four half-square triangle units. Trim all dog ears and press open, with the seams pressed towards the darker fabric.

make 4

MAKING THE FLYING GEESE UNITS

3 Take two colour C 2½in squares and a colour A 2½in x 4½in rectangle and referring to Important Techniques make a flying geese unit. Repeat to make four units.

make 4

PIECING THE BLOCK

4 Join the units together into rows as shown and press. Sew the rows together, pinning at every seam intersection to ensure a perfect match. Piece the centre squares in rows 2 and 3 before sewing the flying geese units to either end. Press rows in alternate directions when possible so seams nest together nicely.

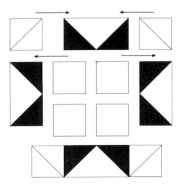

MAKING BLOCK 11 – FAN

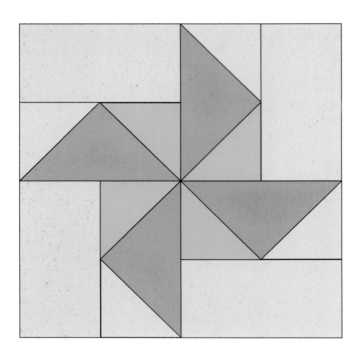

TOTAL STRIPS = 1½
- ¾ colour A strip (mauve).
- ¼ colour B strip (green).
- ½ colour C strip (pink).

CUTTING INSTRUCTIONS
- Colour A – cut four squares 2½in x 2½in and four rectangles 2½in x 4½in.
- Colour B – cut four 2½in squares.
- Colour C – cut four rectangles 2½in x 4½in.

MAKING THE FLYING GEESE UNITS

1 With reference to Important Techniques, take a colour A 2½in square and lay it right sides together with a colour C 2½in x 4½in rectangle. Sew across the diagonal as shown. Flip the square over and press towards the corner.

2 Take a colour C 2½in square and sew to the right-hand side of this unit. Make four of these units.

make 4

PIECING THE BLOCK

3 Sew a colour A rectangle to a flying geese unit as shown below and press.

4 Sew the units together, pinning at every seam intersection to ensure a perfect match.

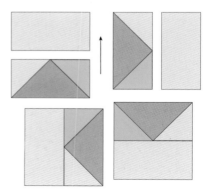

MAKING BLOCK 12 – WATER WHEEL

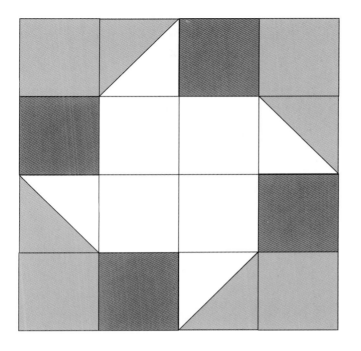

TOTAL STRIPS = 1¼
- ½ colour A strip (yellow).
- ½ colour B strip (aqua).
- ¼ colour C strip (pink).

CUTTING INSTRUCTIONS
- Colour A – from the half strip cut four 2½in squares, set the remaining quarter strip aside for half-square triangle units.
- Colour B – from the half strip cut four 2½in squares, set the remaining quarter strip aside for half-square triangle units.
- Colour C – cut four 2½in squares.

MAKING THE HALF-SQUARE TRIANGLE UNITS

1 Take a colour A quarter strip and a colour B quarter strip and referring to Important Techniques cut four sets of triangles using the Multi-Size 45/90 or other speciality ruler.

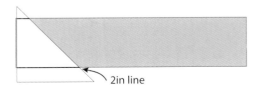

2in line

2 Sew along the diagonals to form four half-square triangle units. Trim dog ears and press open, with the seams pressed towards the darker fabric.

make 4

PIECING THE BLOCK

3 Join the units together into rows and then sew the rows together, pinning at every seam intersection to ensure a perfect match. Press rows in alternate directions wherever possible so seams nest together nicely.

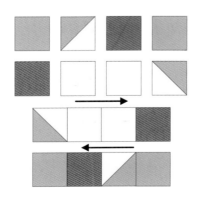

MAKING BLOCK 13 – X-QUARTET

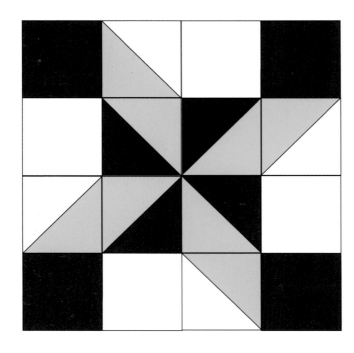

TOTAL STRIPS = 1½
- ½ colour A strip (white).
- ½ colour B strip (green).
- ½ colour C strip (mauve).

CUTTING INSTRUCTIONS
- Colour A – from the half strip cut four 2½in squares, set the remaining quarter strip aside for half-square triangle units.
- Colour B – cut into two separate quarter strips for half-square triangle units.
- Colour C – from the half strip cut four 2½in squares, set the remaining quarter strip aside for half-square triangle units.

MAKING THE HALF-SQUARE TRIANGLE UNITS

1 Take a colour A quarter strip and a colour B quarter strip and referring to Important Techniques cut four sets of triangles using the Multi-Size 45/90 or other speciality ruler.

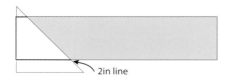

2 Sew along the diagonals to form four half-square triangle units. Trim all dog ears and press open, with the seams pressed towards the darker fabric.

make 4

3 Repeat with the other colour B quarter strip and the colour C quarter strip to make four half-square triangle units.

make 4

PIECING THE BLOCK

4 Join the units together into rows as shown and then sew the rows together, pinning at every seam intersection to ensure a perfect match. Press rows in alternate directions wherever possible so the seams nest together nicely.

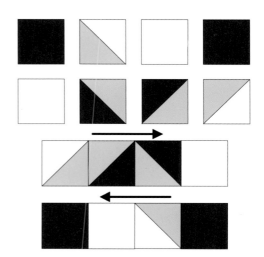

MAKING BLOCK 14 – SHADED TRAIL

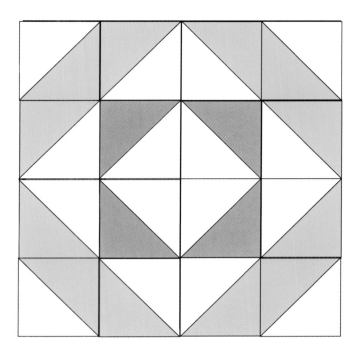

TOTAL STRIPS = 1½
- ¾ colour A strip (white).
- ½ colour B strip (green).
- ¼ colour C strip (pink).

CUTTING INSTRUCTIONS
- Colour A – cut the three-quarter strip into one quarter strip and one half strip.

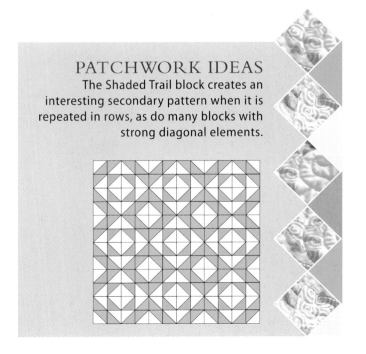

PATCHWORK IDEAS
The Shaded Trail block creates an interesting secondary pattern when it is repeated in rows, as do many blocks with strong diagonal elements.

MAKING THE HALF-SQUARE TRIANGLE UNITS

1 Take the colour A half strip and the colour B half strip and referring to Important Techniques cut twelve sets of triangles using the Multi-Size 45/90 or other speciality ruler.

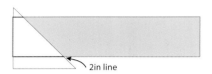

2in line

2 Sew along the diagonals to form twelve half-square triangle units. Trim all dog ears and press open, with the seams pressed towards the darker fabric.

make 12

3 Repeat with the colour A quarter strip and the colour C quarter strip to make four half-square triangle units.

make 4

PIECING THE BLOCK

4 Sew the units together into rows, pinning at every seam intersection to ensure a perfect match. Press rows in alternate directions when possible so seams nest together.

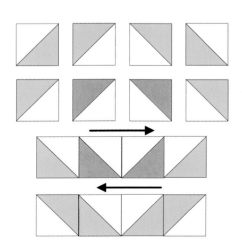

MAKING BLOCK 15 – NELSON'S VICTORY

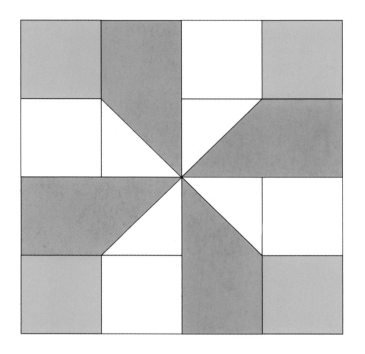

TOTAL STRIPS = 1¼
- ½ colour A strip (white).
- ¼ colour B strip (green).
- ½ colour C strip (pink).

CUTTING INSTRUCTIONS
- Colour A – cut eight 2½in squares.
- Colour B – cut four 2½in squares.
- Colour C – cut four rectangles 2½in x 4½in.

MAKING THE FLYING GEESE UNITS

1 With reference to Important Techniques, take a colour A 2½in square and lay it right sides together with a colour C 2½in x 4½in rectangle. Sew across the diagonal as shown. Flip the square over and press towards the corner. Repeat to make four of these units.

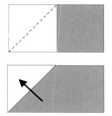

make 4

PIECING THE BLOCK

2 Sew a colour A square to a colour B square and then sew to the flying geese unit, pinning at every seam intersection to ensure a perfect match. Sew the units together.

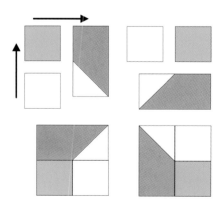

MAKING BLOCK 16 – GEESE IN FLIGHT

TOTAL STRIPS = 1½
- ¾ colour A strip (white).
- ¼ colour B strip (pink).
- ½ colour C strip (aqua).

CUTTING INSTRUCTIONS
- Colour A – cut the three-quarter strip into one quarter strip and one half strip.

MAKING THE HALF-SQUARE TRIANGLE UNITS

1 Take the colour A quarter strip and the colour B quarter strip and referring to Important Techniques cut four sets of triangles using the Multi-Size 45/90 or other speciality ruler.

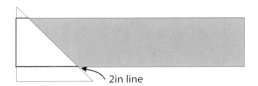

2in line

2 Sew along the diagonals to form four half-square triangle units. Trim all dog ears and press open, with the seams pressed towards the darker fabric.

make 4

3 Repeat with the colour A half strip and the colour C half strip to make twelve half-square triangle units.

make 12

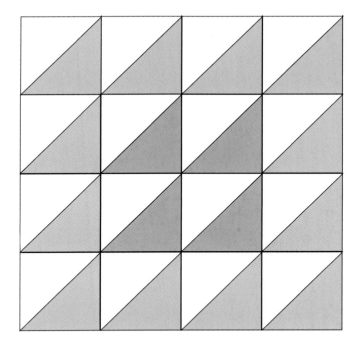

PIECING THE BLOCK

4 Sew the units together, pinning at every seam intersection to ensure a perfect match. Press rows in alternate directions wherever possible so the seams nest together nicely.

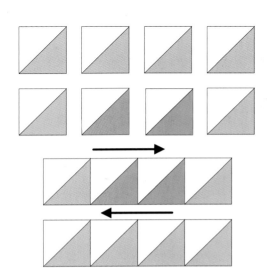

MAKING BLOCK 17 – EVENING STAR

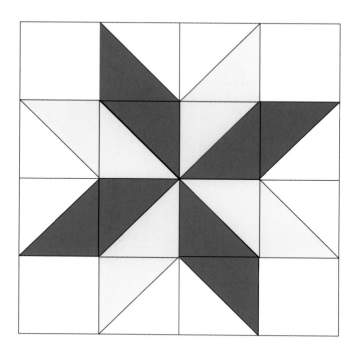

TOTAL STRIPS = 1¾

- ¾ colour A strip (white).
- ½ colour B strip (yellow).
- ½ colour C strip (blue).

CUTTING INSTRUCTIONS

- Colour A – cut the three-quarter strip into three separate quarter strips,
  set two aside for half-square triangle units,
  cut the remaining quarter strip into four 2½in squares.
- Colour B – cut the half strip into two separate quarter strips for half-square triangle units.
- Colour C – cut the half strip into two separate quarter strips for half-square triangle units.

MAKING THE HALF-SQUARE TRIANGLE UNITS

1 Take a colour A quarter strip and a colour B quarter strip and referring to Important Techniques cut four sets of triangles using the Multi-Size 45/90 or other speciality ruler.

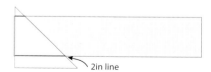

2 Sew along the diagonals to form four half-square triangle units. Trim dog ears and press open, with the seams pressed towards the darker fabric.

make 4

3 Repeat with the other colour A quarter strip and the colour C quarter strip to make another four half-square triangle units.

make 4

4 Repeat with the other colour B quarter strip and the other colour C quarter strip to make another four half-square triangle units.

make 4

PIECING THE BLOCK

5 Join the units together and then sew the rows together, pinning at seam intersections to ensure a perfect match. Press rows in alternate directions where possible so seams nest together nicely.

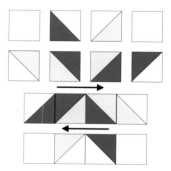

MAKING BLOCK 18 – MARTHA WASHINGTON STAR

TOTAL STRIPS = 1¾
- 1 colour A strip (white).
- ¼ colour B strip (pink).
- ½ colour C strip (aqua).

CUTTING INSTRUCTIONS
- Colour A – cut four 2½in squares and six rectangles 2½in x 4½in.
- Colour B – cut four 2½in squares.
- Colour C – cut eight 2½in squares.

MAKING THE FLYING GEESE UNITS

1 Take two colour B 2½in squares and a colour A 2½in x 4½in rectangle and following Important Techniques make a flying geese unit. Repeat to make two units.

make 2

2 Take two colour C 2½in squares and a colour A 2½in x 4½in rectangle and make a flying geese unit. Repeat to make four units.

make 4

PIECING THE BLOCK

3 Join the units together and then sew the rows together, pinning at seam intersections to ensure a perfect match. Piece the centre flying geese units in rows 2 and 3 before sewing the flying geese units to both ends. Press rows in alternate directions where possible so seams nest together.

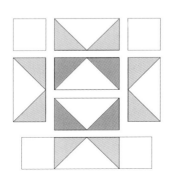

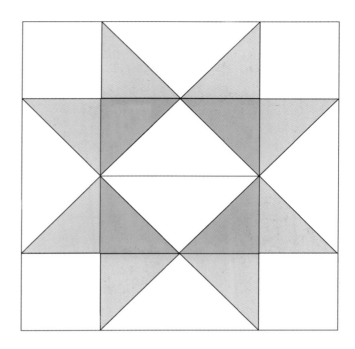

ASSEMBLING THE QUILT

SEWING THE BLOCKS TOGETHER

1 Referring to the diagram below join the blocks together to form rows, alternating the snowball blocks with the sampler blocks, making sure you position the snowball blocks correctly to create the pattern. Always press towards the sampler blocks and your seams will nest together nicely. Pin at every seam intersection to ensure a perfect match.

ADDING THE BORDER

2 Determine the horizontal measurement from side to side across the centre of the quilt top. Cut two border strips to this measurement. Sew to the top and bottom of your quilt. Adding these borders first avoids having a join in them.

3 Join the remaining four border strips to form two lengths. Determine the vertical measurement from top to bottom across the centre of your quilt top. Cut two side borders to this measurement and sew to the quilt. Your quilt top is now complete. Quilt as desired – see Quilting.

4 Bind the quilt to finish – see Binding a Quilt. To create a scrappy binding, cut each binding strip into four quarters (approximately 2½in x 10½in). Sew the quarters into a continuous length making sure you don't have similar fabrics next to each other.

Our variation quilt was made by Gill Penn who works in The Quilt Room – another willing volunteer who succumbed to a bit of arm twisting! She chose a range from Kansas Troubles called Summer's End, which contains gorgeous earthy colours of dark blues, reds and greens mixed with shades of cream running through to tan. The quilt was longarm quilted by The Quilt Room.

STAR
SAMPLER QUILT

Over the years star blocks have been designed in many forms and variations and in this elegant quilt we used nine different star blocks. A taupe Jelly Roll™ was the starting point and a combination of three different size blocks – 16in, 12in and 8in. We had great fun with this quilt and seem to be perfecting the art of making our Jelly Rolls™ go further! We decided to create a more uniform look by using the same additional background fabric in each block to replace the light fabric. We also made use of our additional background fabric by allowing ourselves the luxury of four 4½in wide strips which we used in several of our blocks as squares and triangles. This fabric is listed separately.

The lovely variation quilt shown at the end of the chapter uses reproduction 1930s fabrics to create a sunny quilt with a hint of nostalgia.

STAR SAMPLER QUILT

VITAL STATISTICS

QUILT SIZE	60in x 60in
BLOCK SIZE	8in, 12in and 16in square
BLOCKS PER QUILT	29
SETTING	one 16in centre block, twelve 8in blocks in first border, 2in second border, sixteen 12in blocks in third border

REQUIREMENTS

- One Jelly Roll™
- 3¼yd (3m) of background and inner border fabric
- 20in (50cm) of binding fabric
- Multi-Size 45/90 ruler or other speciality tool for making half-square triangles

SORTING YOUR JELLY ROLL STRIPS

- Sort your strips before you start your quilt. Each block gives its own strip requirements but it is important to sort them before you start and label the strips once sorted.
- In this quilt your background fabric becomes the light in every block. Be prepared to play around with your Jelly Roll™ strips until you are happy with the results.
- Note: when you need more than one strip for a colour, i.e., one and a half strips for the centre block, you need to make sure they look similar – you don't want one strip of a red and a half strip of a blue. Select one strip of a red and then a half strip of another red.
- Choose the strips for the 12in blocks before choosing the strips for the twelve 8in Stardust blocks. This will give you more choice of colour for your 12in blocks.
- Twelve different strips are required for the twelve Stardust blocks although only a three-quarter strip is needed for each block. You therefore have twelve quarter strips spare. Don't discard these as they are used in other blocks as offcuts.
- Refer to the Cutting Chart opposite which gives the strips required for each block and any offcuts used, together with the number of each block to be made.

CUTTING INSTRUCTIONS

Background fabric:

- Cut thirty-seven 2½in wide strips across the width of the fabric. Set aside five strips for the inner border. The remaining thirty-two strips will be required for the blocks.
- Cut four 4½in wide strips. Subcut two strips into fourteen 4½in squares. Leave the other two strips uncut to be used in the Twinkling Star block.

Binding fabric:

- Cut six 2½in wide strips across the width of the fabric.

CUTTING CHART FOR THE STAR SAMPLER QUILT

This table shows the number of Jelly Roll™ and background strips for each block and the number of blocks that need to be made. It is important to select all your strips at the start and label them. The offcuts are all taken from the twelve strips allocated for the twelve Stardust blocks as only a three-quarter strip is required for each block.

BLOCK	JELLY ROLL COLOUR A	JELLY ROLL COLOUR B	JELLY ROLL STRIPS PER BLOCK	NO. OF BLOCKS TO MAKE	TOTAL JELLY ROLL STRIPS PER QUILT	BACKGROUND 2½IN STRIPS PER BLOCK	BACKGROUND 2½IN STRIPS PER QUILT	BACKGROUND EXTRA
1 Twinkling Star 16in	1½		1½	1	1½	½	½	Two 4½in wide strips
2 Stardust 8in	1		1	12	12	¾	9	
3 Crow's Foot 12in	1½	¼ offcut	1½ + ¼ offcut	4	6 + four ¼ offcuts	1	4	Eight 4½in squares
4 Rising Star 12in	2		2	2	4	1½	3	Two 4½in squares
5 Cup and Saucer 12in	1¾	¼ offcut	1¾ + ¼ offcut	2	3½	1½	3	
6 Eddystone Light 12in	2		2	2	4	1½	3	Two 4½in squares
7 Amish Star 12in	1	½	1½	2	3	1½	3	
8 Love in the Mist 12in	1½		1½	2	3	1¾	3½	Two 4½in squares
9 Indian Hatchet 12in	1	½ + two ¼ offcuts	1½ + two ¼ offcuts	2	3 + four ¼ offcuts	1½	3	
TOTAL					**40 Jelly Roll™ strips**		**32 background strips**	**Two 4½in wide strips plus fourteen 4½in squares**

MAKING CENTRE BLOCK 1 – TWINKLING STAR 16IN

TOTAL STRIPS = 2

- 1½ colour A strips (red).
- ½ background 2½in strip.
- 2 background 4½in strips.

CUTTING INSTRUCTIONS

- Background – cut four 4½in squares from one 4½in wide strip. Set aside the other 4½in strip for cutting the 4in finished triangles.

MAKING THE HALF-SQUARE TRIANGLE UNITS

1 Take the colour A half strip and the background half strip and, referring to Important Techniques, cut twelve sets of triangles using the Multi-Size 45/90 or other speciality ruler.

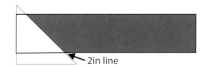

2in line

2 Sew along the diagonals to form twelve half-square triangle units. Trim all dog ears and press open with the seams pressed towards the darker fabric.

make 12

MAKING THE COLOUR A TRIANGLES

3 Take the colour A strip and using the Multi-Size 45/90 cut twenty-four 2in finished triangles.

make 24

MAKING THE BACKGROUND TRIANGLES

4 Take the background 4½in strip and using the Multi-Size 45/90 with the 4in line on the bottom of the strip, cut twelve 4in finished triangles.

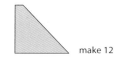

make 12

PIECING THE BLOCK

5 Sew a colour A 2in triangle to the right side of the half-square triangle unit as shown. Press towards the triangle.

6 Sew a colour A 2in triangle to the top of this unit as shown.

7 Sew a background 4in triangle to this unit and press to the background triangle. Repeat to make twelve units.

8 Join the units together and then sew the rows together, pinning at seam intersections to ensure a perfect match. Press rows in alternate directions wherever possible so the seams nest together nicely.

MAKING BLOCK 2 – STARDUST 8IN

TOTAL STRIPS = 1½

- ¾ colour A strip (grey).
- ¾ of a background 2½in strip.
- note: one Jelly Roll™ strip has been allocated for each block so you will have 12 quarter strips spare. Do not discard these as you will need to use them in other blocks.

CUTTING INSTRUCTIONS FOR EACH BLOCK
You need to make twelve Stardust blocks for the quilt.

- Colour A – cut twelve 2½in squares.
- Background – cut four 2½in squares and four 2½in x 4½in rectangles.

MAKING THE FLYING GEESE UNITS

1 Take two colour A 2½in squares and a background 2½in x 4½in rectangle and following Important Techniques make a flying geese unit. Repeat to make four of these units.

make 4

PIECING THE BLOCK

2 Sew the centre squares together and sew a flying geese unit to both sides as shown below. Press seams towards the centre.

3 Sew a background square to each side of two flying geese units and press towards the squares.

4 Join the units together, pinning at every seam intersection to ensure a perfect match.

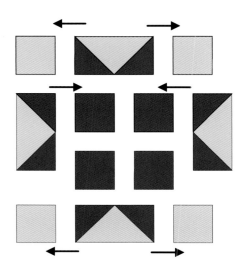

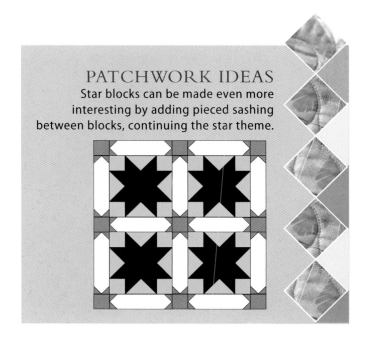

PATCHWORK IDEAS
Star blocks can be made even more interesting by adding pieced sashing between blocks, continuing the star theme.

MAKING CORNER BLOCK 3 – CROW'S FOOT 12IN

TOTAL STRIPS = 2¾
- 1½ colour A strip (brown).
- ¼ strip offcut.
- 1 background strip.
- plus two 4½in background squares.

CUTTING INSTRUCTIONS
You need to make four Crow's Foot blocks for the quilt.
- Colour A – from the half strip cut six 2½in squares.
  Set the other strip aside for half-square triangle units.
- Offcut – cut four 2½in squares.
- Background – cut two 2½in squares and set the rest of the
  strip aside for half-square triangle units.

MAKING THE HALF-SQUARE TRIANGLE UNITS

1 Take a colour A strip and the balance of the background strip and, referring to Important Techniques, cut sixteen sets of triangles using the Multi-Size 45/90 or other speciality ruler.

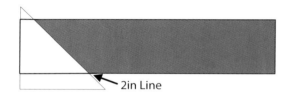

2 Sew along the diagonals to form sixteen half-square triangle units. Trim all dog ears and press open with the seams pressed towards the darker fabric.

make 16

PIECING THE BLOCK

3 Sew the quarters of the block together as shown below, pinning at every seam intersection to ensure a perfect match.

4 Sew the quarters together pressing seams in alternate directions wherever possible so the seams nest together nicely.

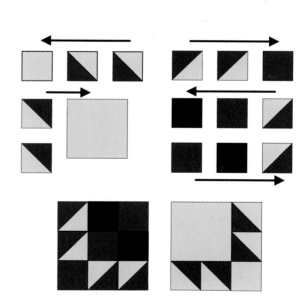

MAKING BLOCK 4 – RISING STAR 12IN

TOTAL STRIPS = 3½

- 2 colour A strips (brown).
- 1½ background strips.
- plus a 4½in background square.

CUTTING INSTRUCTIONS
You need to make two Rising Star blocks for the quilt.

- Colour A – from one strip cut eight 2½in x 4½in rectangles.
  – from the other strip cut eight 2½in squares and set the remainder aside for half-square triangles.
- Background – from the full strip cut sixteen 2½in squares.

MAKING THE HALF-SQUARE TRIANGLE UNITS

1 Take the balance of the colour A strip allocated for half-square triangles and the background half strip and, referring to Important Techniques, cut eight sets of triangles using the Multi-Size 45/90 or other speciality ruler.

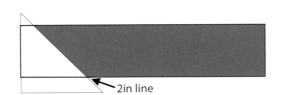

2in line

2 Sew along the diagonals to form eight half-square triangle units. Trim all dog ears and press open with the seams pressed towards the darker fabric.

make 8

MAKING THE FLYING GEESE UNITS

3 Take two 2½in background squares and a Colour A 2½in x 4½in rectangle and following Important Techniques make a flying geese unit. Repeat to make eight units.

make 8

PIECING THE BLOCK

4 Sew the flying geese units together and press as shown in the diagram below.

5 Sew the corner units together and press as shown, pinning at seam intersections to ensure a perfect match.

6 Sew the units into rows and sew the rows together, pressing rows in alternate directions wherever possible so the seams nest together nicely.

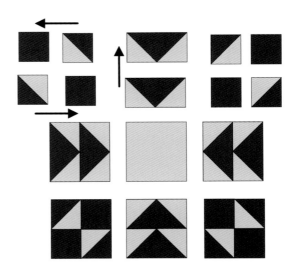

MAKING BLOCK 5 – CUP AND SAUCER 12IN

TOTAL STRIPS = 3½

- 1¾ colour A strip (brown).
- ¼ strip offcut.
- 1½ background strips.

CUTTING INSTRUCTIONS

You need to make two Cup and Saucer blocks for the quilt.

- Colour A – from the full strip cut sixteen 2½in squares.
  – from the three-quarters strip cut four 2½in squares. Set the remainder of the strip aside for half-square triangles.
  – from the quarter strip offcut cut four 2½in squares.
- Background – from the full strip cut eight 2½in x 4½in rectangles and two 2½in squares.
  – from the half strip cut two 2½in squares. Set the remainder aside for half-square triangle units.

MAKING THE HALF-SQUARE TRIANGLE UNITS

1 Take the balance of the colour A strip and the balance of the background strip and, referring to Important Techniques, cut eight sets of triangles using the Multi-Size 45/90 or other speciality ruler.

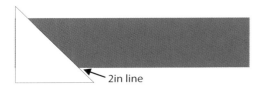

2in line

2 Sew along the diagonals to form eight half-square triangle units. Trim all dog ears and press open with the seams pressed towards the darker fabric.

  make 8

MAKING THE FLYING GEESE UNITS

3 Take two colour A 2½in squares and a background 2½in x 4½in rectangle and following Important Techniques make a flying geese unit. Repeat to make eight units.

 make 8

PIECING THE BLOCK

4 Sew the flying geese units together and press as shown. Sew the corner units together and press as shown, pinning at every seam intersection to ensure a perfect match.

5 Sew the units into rows and sew the rows together, pressing rows in alternate directions wherever possible so the seams nest together nicely.

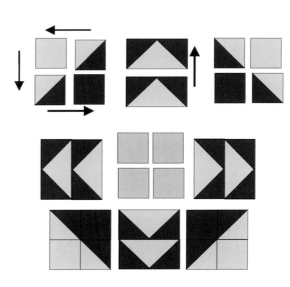

MAKING BLOCK 6 – EDDYSTONE LIGHT 12IN

TOTAL STRIPS = 3½
- 2 colour A strips (brown).
- 1½ background strips.
- plus one 4½in background square.

CUTTING INSTRUCTIONS
You need to make two Eddystone Light blocks for the quilt.
- Colour A – from the two strips cut twenty-four 2½in squares and four rectangles 2½in x 4½in.
- Background – cut eight rectangles 2½in x 4½in from one strip and eight 2½in squares from the half strip.

MAKING THE FLYING GEESE UNITS

1 Take two colour A 2½in squares and a background 2½in x 4½in rectangle and following Important Techniques make a flying geese unit. Repeat to make eight of these units.

make 8

2 Repeat the step above with background squares sewn on to colour A rectangles. Make four of these units.

make 4

PIECING THE BLOCK

3 Sew a flying geese unit to both sides of the centre unit and press to the centre as shown in the diagram below.

4 Sew the squares to both sides of two flying geese units, pressing to the squares and sew to the top and bottom of the centre unit.

5 Sew the outer side flying geese units and sew to both sides of the centre unit.

6 Join the top and bottom rows and sew to the top and bottom of the centre unit, pinning at every seam intersection to ensure a perfect match.

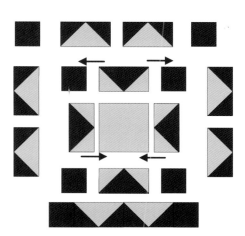

MAKING BLOCK 7 – AMISH STAR 12IN

TOTAL STRIPS = 3
- 1 colour A strip (brown).
- ½ colour B strip (black).
- 1½ background strips.

CUTTING INSTRUCTIONS
You need to make two Amish Star blocks for the quilt.
- Colour A –cut eight 2½in squares and set the remaining half strip aside for half-square triangle units.
- Colour B – cut four 2½in x 4½in rectangles.
- Background – from one strip cut eight 2½in squares and four 2½in x 4½in rectangles. Set the other half strip aside for half-square triangle units.

MAKING THE HALF-SQUARE TRIANGLE UNITS
1 Take a colour A half strip and a background half strip and, referring to Important Techniques, cut twelve sets of triangles using the Multi-Size 45/90 or other speciality ruler.

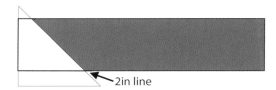

2in line

2 Sew along the diagonals to form twelve half-square triangle units. Trim all dog ears and press open with the seams pressed towards the darker fabric.

make 12

MAKING THE FLYING GEESE UNITS
3 Take two background 2½in squares and a colour B 2½in x 4½in rectangle and following Important Techniques make a flying geese unit. Repeat to make four of these units.

make 4

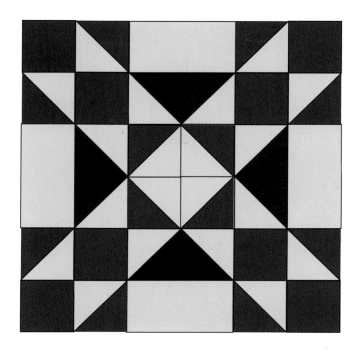

PIECING THE BLOCK
4 Sew the centre unit together and press as shown in the diagram below.

5 Sew the flying geese units and the background rectangles together and press as shown below.

6 Sew the corner units together and press as shown, pinning at seam intersections to ensure a perfect match.

7 Sew the units into rows and sew the rows together, pressing rows in alternate directions wherever possible so the seams nest together nicely.

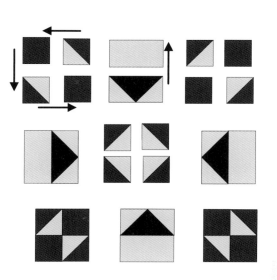

MAKING BLOCK 8 – LOVE IN THE MIST 12IN

TOTAL STRIPS = 3¼
- 1½ colour A strip (brown).
- 1¾ background strip.
- plus a 4½in background square.

CUTTING INSTRUCTIONS:
You need to make two Love in the Mist blocks for the quilt.
- Colour A – from the whole strip cut eight 2½in x 4½in rectangles and two 2½in squares.
  – from the half strip cut two 2½in squares and set the remainder aside for half-square triangles.
- Background – cut twenty 2½in squares and set the remainder aside for half-square triangles

MAKING THE HALF-SQUARE TRIANGLE UNITS

1 Take the balance of the colour A half strip and the balance of the background strips and, referring to Important Techniques, cut eight sets of triangles using the Multi-Size 45/90 or other speciality ruler.

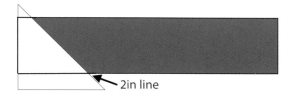

2in line

2 Sew along the diagonals to form eight half-square triangle units. Trim all dog ears and press open with the seams pressed towards the darker fabric.

make 8

MAKING THE FLYING GEESE UNITS

3 Take two background 2½in squares and a colour A 2½in x 4½in rectangle and following Important Techniques make a flying geese unit. Repeat to make eight units.

make 8

PIECING THE BLOCK

4 Sew the flying geese units together as shown in the diagram below. Sew the corner units together as shown, pinning at every seam intersection to ensure a perfect match. Press the work.

5 Sew the units together into rows and then sew the rows together. Press rows in alternate directions wherever possible so the seams nest together nicely.

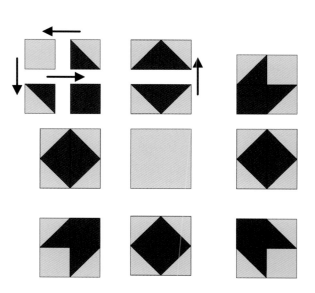

MAKING BLOCK 9 – INDIAN HATCHET 12IN

TOTAL STRIPS = 3½
- 1 colour A strip (brown).
- ½ colour B strip (red).
- two ¼ strip offcuts, preferably a light and a dark.
- 1½ background strips.

CUTTING INSTRUCTIONS
You need to make two Indian Hatchet blocks for the quilt.
- Colour B – cut into eight 2½in squares.
- Background – cut the half strip into four 2½in x 4½in rectangles.

MAKING THE HALF-SQUARE TRIANGLE UNITS

1 Take the colour A strip and the background strip and, referring to Important Techniques, cut twenty-four sets of triangles using the Multi-Size 45/90 or other speciality ruler.

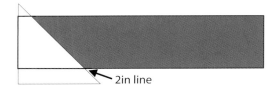

2in line

2 Sew along the diagonals to form twenty-four half-square triangle units. Trim all dog ears and press open with the seams pressed towards the darker fabric.

make 24

3 Repeat with the two offcut quarter strips to create four half-square triangle units.

make 4

MAKING THE FLYING GEESE UNITS

4 Take two Colour B squares and a background rectangle and following Important Techniques make a flying geese unit. Repeat to make four units.

make 4

PIECING THE BLOCK

5 Join the units together into rows as shown below and then sew the rows together, pinning at every seam intersection to ensure a perfect match.

6 Piece the centre squares in rows 3 and 4 before sewing the flying geese units to either end. Press rows in alternate directions wherever possible so the seams nest together nicely.

ASSEMBLING THE QUILT

SEWING YOUR BLOCKS TOGETHER

1 Sew two pairs of Stardust blocks together and sew to either side of the central Twinkling Star block, as shown right.

2 Sew four Stardust blocks together and sew to the top of the quilt. Sew another four Stardust blocks together and sew to the bottom of the quilt.

ADDING THE INNER BORDER

3 Determine the vertical measurement from top to bottom of the quilt top. Cut two inner border strips to this measurement and sew to either side of the quilt, as shown right, pinning and easing where necessary.

4 Join the remaining three inner border strips into one continuous length. Determine the horizontal measurement from side to side through the centre of your quilt top. Cut two lengths to this measurement and sew to the top and bottom of the quilt, pinning and easing where necessary. Your quilt top should now measure 36½in square. Press the work.

5 Lay out the 12in blocks into a pleasing arrangement with a Crow's Foot block at each corner. Sew three blocks together and sew to one side of the quilt top. Repeat and sew three blocks to the other side. Press the work.

6 Sew five blocks together and sew to the top of the quilt. Repeat and sew five blocks to the bottom of the quilt. Press the work.

7 Your quilt top is now complete. Quilt as desired and bind to finish – see Quilting and Binding a Quilt.

Our variation was made by Kath Bock and Vivian de Lang using a reproduction thirties Jelly Roll™ with a white on white background. A 4in wide border was added to increase the size of the quilt to 68in x 68in. You will need an extra 27in cut into six 4½in strips for the border. You will also need one extra 2½in strip for your binding. The quilt was longarm quilted by The Quilt Room in a pretty thirties flower design.

BASKET
SAMPLER QUILT

Basket blocks are very popular and there are a surprising number of them, so we thought a collection of different baskets would make a lovely sampler quilt. For the quilt shown here we used a classic combination of blue and white and arranged the blocks on point for a dynamic look.

The beauty of this Basket Sampler Quilt is that all the cutting is done at the beginning, which makes for a lot of speedy cutting of squares, rectangles and half-square triangles before starting to sew the quilt. All you then have to do is to follow the piecing diagrams to make two each of the nine basket blocks. We have allowed extra half-square triangle units to give you some flexibility in your design.

Look at the gorgeous variation quilt at the end of this chapter to see how different this quilt can appear using a range of multicoloured 1940s fabrics.

BASKET SAMPLER QUILT

VITAL STATISTICS

QUILT SIZE	62in x 82in
BLOCK SIZE	10in square plus 2in frame
BLOCKS PER QUILT	18
SETTING	3 x 4 blocks on point

REQUIREMENTS

- One Jelly Roll™
- 3¾yd (3.5m) of light fabric
- 24in (60cm) of fabric for for binding
- Multi-Size 45/90 or other speciality ruler for making half-square triangles

SORTING YOUR JELLY ROLL STRIPS

As we are adding additional light fabric to our Jelly Roll™, we only have to sort our Jelly Roll™ into medium and dark fabrics. Be guided by what is in your roll. Remember this is a scrappy quilt and just about anything will work.

- Choose eight dark strips for the baskets.
- Choose twelve medium strips for the baskets.
- Choose fifteen strips for the framing of the blocks.
- Five strips are spare.
- *Important*: our block diagrams show varying shades of medium colour, to represent the different fabrics that will be used. Your blocks can look even more varied depending on the units you select for your blocks.

CUTTING INSTRUCTIONS FOR JELLY ROLL STRIPS

Baskets:

- Take four medium strips and cut each strip into sixteen 2½in squares. You need fifty-eight in total. Six are spare.
- Take one medium strip and cut into two rectangles 2½in x 4½in and two rectangles 2½in x 8½in.
- Take one dark strip and cut into two rectangles 2½in x 4½in and two rectangles 2½in x 6½in.
- Take one dark strip and cut into sixteen 2½in squares.
- Leave the remaining seven medium and six dark Jelly Roll™ strips uncut.

Block frames:

- Take twelve of the strips allocated for the framing of the blocks and cut each into two rectangles 2½in x 14½in and one rectangle 2½in x 10½in.
- Take the remaining three strips allocated for the framing and cut each into four rectangles 2½in x 10½in to make a total of twenty-four rectangles 2½in x 14½in and twenty-four rectangles 2½in x 10½in.

CUTTING INSTRUCTIONS FOR LIGHT FABRIC

It is important to cut the light fabric in this way to ensure that there is no wastage.

- Cut a length of 46in from the light fabric and cut six strips 2½in wide down the length of the fabric. Cut two 23in squares from the remainder.

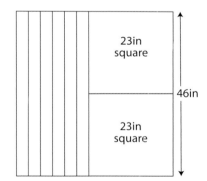

- Cut a length of 25in from the light fabric and cut two 12½in squares and one 23in square as shown.
- Subcut the three 23in squares across both diagonals to

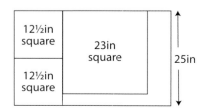

form twelve setting triangles – only ten are needed. Unless you have a very long ruler you will need to use two rulers edged up to each other.

- Subcut across one diagonal of the two 12½in squares to form four corner triangles. Cutting the setting and corner triangles in this way ensures you have no bias edges on the outside of your quilt.

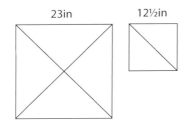

23in   12½in

- Cut a further twenty-one strips 2½in wide across the width of the remainder of the light fabric to make a total of twenty-seven 2½in wide strips. The strips cut lengthways will be a little longer but treat them all the same.

Now subcut the strips as follows:
- Take six strips and cut each into two rectangles 2½in x 14½in and one rectangle 2½in x 10½in.
- Take one strip and cut into four rectangles 2½in x 10½in.
- Take one strip and cut into two rectangles 2½in x 10½in. The balance of this strip can be used later if required. This will make a total of twelve 2½in x 14½in and twelve rectangles 2½in x 10½in for the framing of the six blocks with light fabric frames.
- Take five strips and cut each into six rectangles 2½in x 6½in to make thirty rectangles.
- Take one strip and cut into eight rectangles 2½in x 4½in.
- Take one strip and cut into two rectangles 2½in x 6½in and two rectangles 2½in x 4½in. This will make a total of thirty-two 2½in x 6½in rectangles and a total of ten 2½in x 4½in rectangles.
- Take three strips and cut each into sixteen 2½in squares to make forty-eight 2½in squares (two are spare).
- Leave the remaining nine strips uncut.

Binding:
- Cut eight 2½in wide strips across the width of the fabric.

CUTTING CHART FOR THE BASKET SAMPLER QUILT

Light:	12 – 2½in x 10½in 12 – 2½in x 14½in 32 – 2½in x 6½in 10 – 2½in x 4½in 46 – 2½in x 2½in (+ 2 spare) 9 – uncut strips
Medium:	58 – 2½in x 2½in (+ 6 spare) 2 – 2½in x 4½in 2 – 2½in x 8½in 7 – uncut strips
Dark:	16 – 2½in x 2½in 2 – 2½in x 4½in 2 – 2½in x 6½in 6 – uncut strips
Jelly Roll™ frames:	24 – 2½in x 10½in 24 – 2½in x 14½in

MAKING THE HALF-SQUARE TRIANGLE UNITS

1 Take one medium Jelly Roll™ strip and one light strip and press right sides together ensuring that they are exactly one on top of the other. The pressing will help hold the two strips together. Use the Multi-Size 45/90 and the instructions in Important Techniques to cut the triangles. You need twenty-four sets of triangles per strip.

2 Sew along the diagonals to form a total of twenty-four half-square triangle units. Trim all dog ears and press open with seams pressed towards the darker fabric.

3 Repeat with five medium strips and five light strips to make a total of 120 half-square triangle units in medium and light. Only ninety-eight are needed – twenty-two are spare.

make 98

4 Repeat the above with four dark strips and four light strips to make a total of ninety-six half-square triangle units in dark and light. Only sixty-six are needed – thirty are spare. We found it useful to have extras of the half-square triangle units as we could ring the changes when making some of the duplicate blocks.

make 66

5 Repeat with two dark strips and two medium strips to make a total of forty-eight half-square triangle units in dark and medium. Only forty are needed so eight are spare.

make 40

PIECING THE BLOCKS

6 Referring to the requirements and piecing diagrams for each block (instructions begin overleaf), make two blocks of each basket. The individual units required for each block are also shown.

7 Press frequently as pressing keeps your work accurate. Always set your seams after sewing by pressing the seam as sewn and then pressing on the right side of the fabric towards the darker fabric. When sewing rows together, wherever possible press the seams of alternate rows in opposite directions. This will mean that the seams nest together nicely when sewn together.

8 Pin at every seam intersection to stop any movement when sewing and do not remove the pins too early as your fabric might shift and your seams will not be perfectly aligned.

9 We cannot stress enough the importance of sewing with an accurate scant ¼in seam allowance and would recommend doing a seam allowance test.

PATCHWORK IDEAS

Basket blocks are quite versatile. Try choosing just one basket block from this chapter, make four of them and sew them together, rotating each block 90 degrees to create a pleasing symmetrical design, perhaps the centre for a medallion quilt.

MAKING BLOCK 1 – MAY BASKET

BLOCK REQUIREMENTS

1 Following the diagrams below assemble the following units. These will make one block.

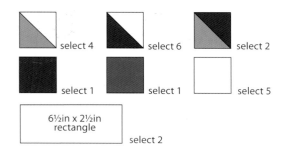

select 4   select 6   select 2

select 1   select 1   select 5

6½in x 2½in rectangle

select 2

PIECING THE BLOCK

2 Sew the squares in the first three rows together and then sew the 6½in light rectangle to the left-hand side.

3 Continue sewing the squares into rows and then sew the rows together, pinning at seam intersections to ensure a perfect match. Press the block. Make two blocks in total.

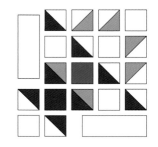

MAKING BLOCK 2 – FLORAL BASKET

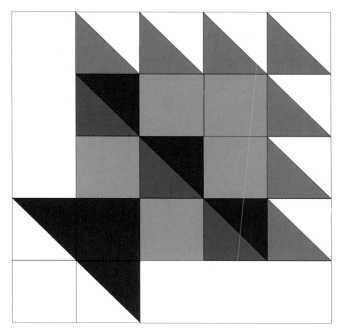

BLOCK REQUIREMENTS

1 Following the diagrams below assemble the following units. These will make one block.

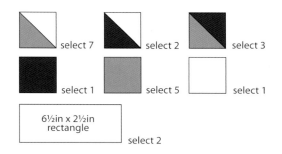

select 7   select 2   select 3

select 1   select 5   select 1

6½in x 2½in rectangle

select 2

PIECING THE BLOCK

2 Sew the squares in the first three rows together and then sew the 6½in light rectangle to the left-hand side.

3 Continue sewing the squares into rows and then sew the rows together, pinning at every seam intersection. Press the block. Make two blocks in total.

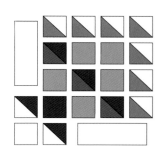

MAKING BLOCK 3 – HANGING BASKET

BLOCK REQUIREMENTS

1 Following the diagrams below assemble the following units. These will make one block.

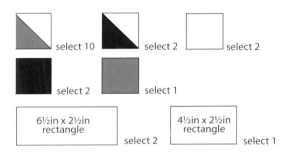

PIECING THE BLOCK

2 Sew the units in the first three rows together and sew the 6½in light rectangle to the left-hand side.

3 Continue sewing the squares into rows and then sew the rows together, pinning at every seam intersection. Press the block. Make two blocks in total.

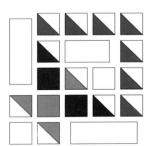

MAKING BLOCK 4 – CHERRY BASKET

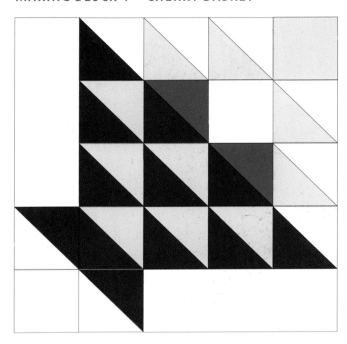

BLOCK REQUIREMENTS

1 Following the diagrams below assemble the following units. These will make one block.

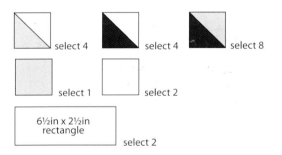

PIECING THE BLOCK

2 Sew the squares in the first three rows together and sew the 6½in light rectangle to the left-hand side.

3 Continue sewing the squares into rows and then sew the rows together, pinning at every seam intersection. Press the block. Make two blocks in total.

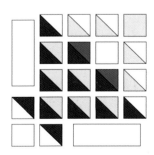

MAKING BLOCK 5 – SEWING BASKET

BLOCK REQUIREMENTS

1 Following the diagrams below assemble the following units. These will make one block.

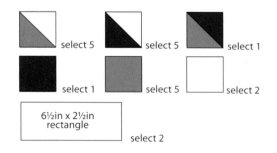

select 5   select 5   select 1

select 1   select 5   select 2

6½in x 2½in rectangle

select 2

PIECING THE BLOCK

2 Sew the squares in the first three rows together and then sew the 6½in light rectangle to the left-hand side.

3 Continue sewing the squares into rows and then sew the rows together, pinning at every seam intersection. Press the block. Make two blocks in total.

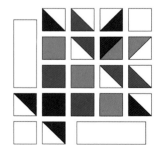

MAKING BLOCK 6 – FRUIT BASKET

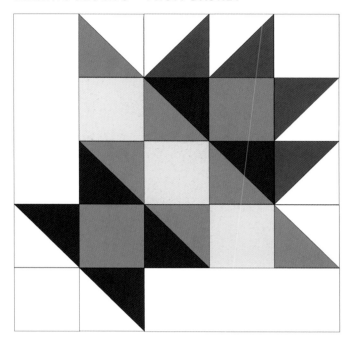

BLOCK REQUIREMENTS

1 Following the diagrams below assemble the following units. These will make one block.

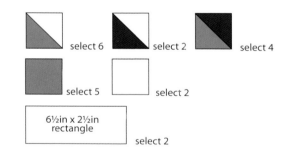

select 6   select 2   select 4

select 5   select 2

6½in x 2½in rectangle

select 2

PIECING THE BLOCK

2 Sew the squares in the first three rows together and then sew the 6½in light rectangle to the left-hand side.

3 Continue sewing the squares into rows and then sew the rows together, pinning at every seam intersection. Press the block. Make two blocks in total.

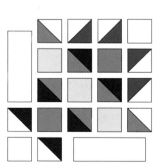

MAKING BLOCK 7 – BREAD BASKET

BLOCK REQUIREMENTS

1 Following the diagrams below assemble the following units. These will make one block.

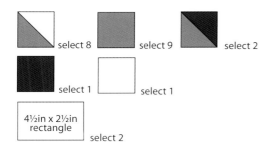

select 8   select 9   select 2   select 1   select 1

4½in x 2½in rectangle   select 2

PIECING THE BLOCK

2 Sew the squares in the first two rows together and then sew the 4½in light rectangle to the left-hand side.

3 Continue sewing the squares into rows and then sew the rows together, pinning at every seam intersection. Press the block. Make two blocks in total.

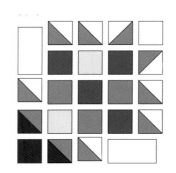

MAKING BLOCK 8 – PICNIC BASKET

BLOCK REQUIREMENTS

1 Following the diagrams below assemble the following units. These will make one block.

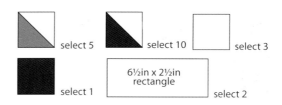

select 5   select 10   select 3   select 1

6½in x 2½in rectangle   select 2

PIECING THE BLOCK

2 Sew the squares in the first three rows together and then sew the 6½in light rectangle to the left-hand side.

3 Continue sewing the squares into rows and then sew the rows together, pinning at every seam intersection. Press the block. Make two blocks in total.

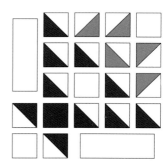

MAKING BLOCK 9 – TULIP BASKET

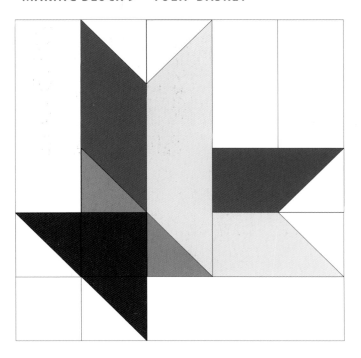

BLOCK REQUIREMENTS

1 Following the diagrams below assemble the following units. These will make one block.

select 2   select 1

select 2   select 5

4½in x 2½in rectangle	
select 2	

6½in x 2½in rectangle	
	select 2

4½in x 2½in rectangle	
select 1	

8½in x 2½in rectangle	
	select 1

select 1

select 1

4½in x 2½in rectangle   6½in x 2½in rectangle

MAKING THE FLIP-OVER CORNERS

2 Lay a 2½in square right sides together on the rectangle. Sew across the diagonal and then flip the square over and press. Trim the excess fabric from the square but do not trim the rectangle as this will keep your work in shape. You can draw the diagonal line on the wrong side of the square or mark it with a fold to help keep your sewing accurate. Repeat this process wherever a flip-over corner is required.

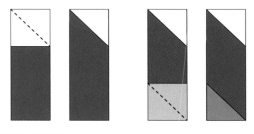

PIECING THE BLOCK

3 Sew the units together as shown below, pinning at every seam intersection to ensure a perfect match. Press the block. Make two blocks in total.

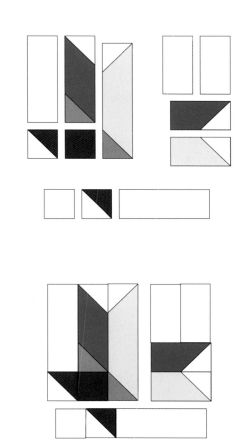

ADDING THE BLOCK FRAMES

1 Light frames have to be added to six of the inner blocks and Jelly Roll™ frames have to be added to twelve blocks. It is therefore necessary to lay out the blocks as shown in the quilt diagram below to find an arrangement you are happy with before sewing on the correct frames.

2 When you have decided on your layout, sew a 10½in long framing strip to the sides of the block and a 14½in framing strip to the top and bottom. When adding the Jelly Roll™ frames, use a different Jelly Roll™ strip on each side of the block. Six blocks require light frames and twelve blocks require Jelly Roll™ frames.

ASSEMBLING THE QUILT

3 Sew a setting triangle to each side of a block to create row 1, as shown below. The setting triangles have been cut slightly larger to make the blocks 'float', so when sewing the setting triangles make sure the bottom of the triangle is aligned with the block. Press as shown.

4 Continue to sew the blocks together to form rows with setting triangles at each end. Press as shown. Sew the rows together, pinning at every intersection. Sew the corner triangles on last.

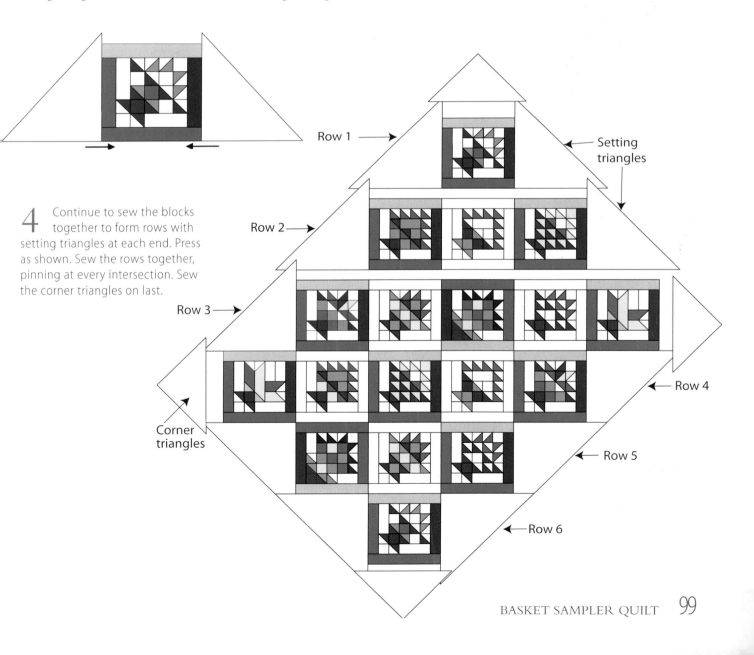

3 Your quilt top is now complete. Quilt as desired and bind to finish – see Quilting and Binding a Quilt. We used a swirly pattern to contrast with the linear elements of the patchwork, with a dark blue for the binding to frame the whole quilt.

*How about this for a gorgeous variation? The range of fabrics is Punctuation by American Jane for Moda and, yes, we love it!
The dotty red background sets off the blocks perfectly. The quilt was made by Ileana Laws and longarm quilted by The Quilt
Room. We chose a fun quilting design that works well with the 1940s prints.*

PICK 'N' MIX
QUILTS

The sampler quilts in this book have given you all the information you need to make an exciting variety of 8in, 10in, 12in and 16in blocks – see the Block Library for a quick reference on what blocks are available to you. If you think of these blocks as ingredients and you have a store cupboard of forty Jelly Roll™ strips, you can then choose different blocks and create your own recipe for a Jelly Roll™ quilt.

Of course, you are not just restricted to sampler quilts, you can pick and mix your way to enormous fun and variation. In this section we show you how to make five quilts but these are just the starting point. You will soon be concocting recipes for other delicious Jelly Roll™ quilts. It's all very addictive but luckily very light on calories! Let these quilts be just the starting point – be inspired and be adventurous.

FRUIT SALAD QUILT

REQUIREMENTS

- One Jelly Roll™ OR forty 2½in wide strips
- 1½yd (1.2m) border fabric cut into five 8½in wide strips across the fabric width
- Binding made from spare strips and offcuts

VITAL STATISTICS

QUILT SIZE	56in x 56in
BLOCK SIZES	8in and 12in
BLOCKS PER QUILT	4 Rolling Pinwheel and 16 Friendship Star + 8in wide border

TOTAL STRIPS = 38

- Four 12in Rolling Pinwheel blocks of 3½ strips each = 14 strips.
- Sixteen 8in Friendship Star blocks of 1½ strips each = 24 strips.

SORTING YOUR JELLY ROLL STRIPS

- Four 12in Rolling Pinwheel blocks create the centre of this quilt, measuring 24in square and using up fourteen strips.
- Friendship Star blocks surround the centre – three 8in blocks on each side to sew to our 24in centre, plus four corners. This meant we needed sixteen Friendship Star blocks in total and as they required one and a half strips each we used up another twenty-four strips. We had now used thirty-eight strips which meant we had two spare.
- You will need a Jelly Roll™ that has lots of lights and the one that we used from Fig Tree Quilts was perfect. Be prepared to make some of your blocks scrappy if you are a bit low on lights.
- When making multiple blocks from the same design you will find you don't use as much fabric as that needed for just one block. We had sufficient fabric over to add to our two spare strips to make a pretty, scrappy binding.

The Rolling Pinwheel block is used in the Classic Sampler Quilt and we've used four for the centre of this quilt. This block is easy to piece and creates a great secondary pattern when sewn together. The centre is then surrounded by 8in Friendship Star blocks, first used in the Snowball Sampler Quilt. A wide 8in border sets off the design.

MAKING THE QUILT

1 Follow the instructions for making the 12in Rolling Pinwheel block to make four in total.

Rolling Pinwheel block

2 Follow the instructions for making the 8in Friendship Star block to make sixteen in total.

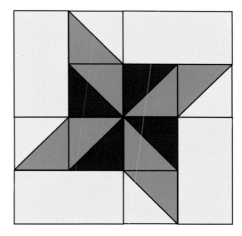

Friendship Star block

3 Sew the four Rolling Pinwheel blocks together and press. Sew three Friendship Star blocks together and sew to the top of the quilt. Pin well at seam intersections to ensure a perfect match. Repeat to sew three Friendship Star blocks to the bottom of the quilt.

4 Now sew five Friendship Star blocks together and sew to one side of the quilt and repeat to sew five blocks to the other side of the quilt.

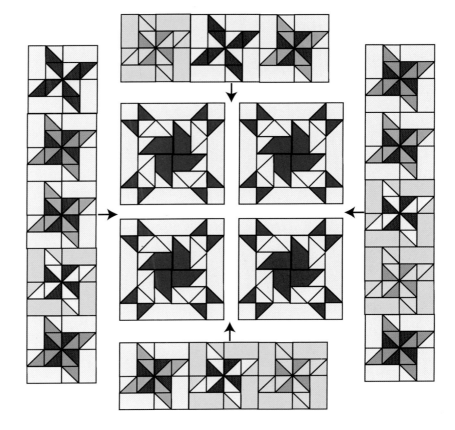

5 Sew the border strips into a continuous length and add to the quilt – see Adding Borders for instructions.

6 Your quilt top is now complete. Quilt as desired and bind to finish – see Quilting and Binding a Quilt. We used a floral rose quilting design on our quilt.

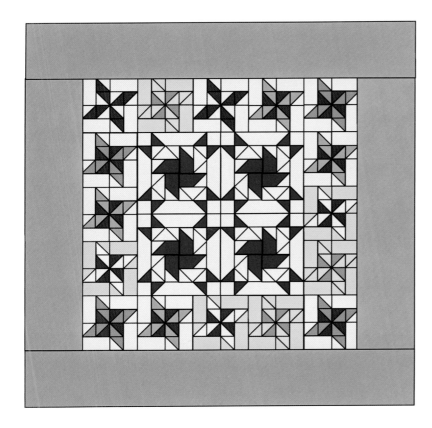

LIQUORICE STICKS QUILT

VITAL STATISTICS

QUILT SIZE   40in x 52in
BLOCK SIZE   12in
BLOCKS PER QUILT 6 Rolling Stone and 6 Tulip
SETTING   3 x 4 blocks with 2½in wide border

REQUIREMENTS

- One Jelly Roll™ OR forty 2½in wide strips
- 16in (40cm) of border fabric cut into five 2½in wide strips across the fabric width
- 16in (40cm) of binding fabric cut into five 2½in wide strips across the fabric width

TOTAL STRIPS = 42

- Six 12in Rolling Stone blocks of 3½ strips each = 21 strips.
- Six 12in Tulip blocks of 3½ strips each = 21 strips.
- Don't panic – you have plenty of fabric in one Jelly Roll™.

SORTING YOUR JELLY ROLL STRIPS

- When making multiple blocks of the same design you don't use as much fabric as needed for just one block, so you will have sufficient. You will find you use less dark strips for the centre squares in the Rolling Stone block plus there are lots of offcuts from the dark strips in the Tulip block.

MAKING THE QUILT

1 Follow the instructions for making the 12in Rolling Stone block to make six blocks in total.

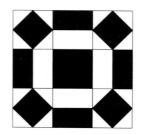

Rolling Stone block

2 Follow the instructions for making the 12in Tulip block to make six blocks in total.

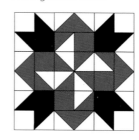

Tulip block

3 Lay out the blocks as shown and when happy with the layout sew them into rows. Sew the rows together, pinning at seam intersections to ensure a perfect match.

4 Sew the border strips into a continuous length and sew to the quilt – see Adding Borders.

5 Your quilt top is now complete. Quilt as desired and bind to finish – see Quilting and Binding a Quilt.

The Rolling Stone block is a wonderful block to alternate with any other block as it creates so much movement. It is used here with the Tulip block and a stunning black and white Jelly Roll™. These blocks were used in the Classic Sampler Quilt.

RHUBARB AND CUSTARD QUILT

VITAL STATISTICS

QUILT SIZE	48in x 56in
BLOCK SIZE	8in
BLOCKS PER QUILT	8 King's Crown, 8 Fox and Geese and 8 Shaded Trail
SETTING	4 x 5 blocks with 8in wide border with four corner blocks

REQUIREMENTS

- One Jelly Roll™ OR forty 2½in wide strips
- 1yd (1m) of border fabric cut into four 8½in wide strips across the fabric width
- 20in (50cm) of binding fabric cut into six 2½in wide strips across the fabric width

TOTAL STRIPS = 40

- Eight 8in King's Crown blocks of 1½ strips each = 12 strips.
- Eight 8in Fox and Geese blocks of 2 strips each = 16 strips.
- Eight 8in Shaded Trail blocks of 1½ strips each = 12 strips.

MAKING THE QUILT

1 Follow the instructions for making the 8in King's Crown block to make eight in total. Four of these are used in the outer border.

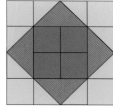
King's Crown block

2 Follow the instructions for making the 8in Fox and Geese block to make eight in total.

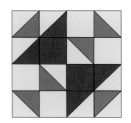
Fox and Geese block

3 Follow the instructions for making the 8in Shaded Trail block to make eight in total.

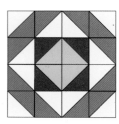
Shaded Trail block

4 Lay out the blocks as shown below and sew them into rows. Sew the rows together, pinning at seam intersections to ensure a perfect match.

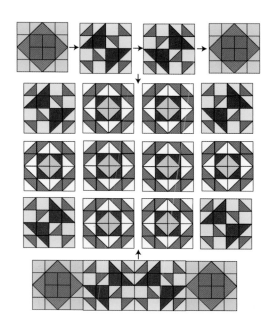

5 Measure your quilt to calculate the border – see Adding Borders. Sew the border strips to the quilt with the remaining four King's Crown blocks at each corner.

6 Your quilt top is now complete. Quilt as desired and bind to finish – see Quilting and Binding a Quilt. We chose a large daisy design to quilt in the borders.

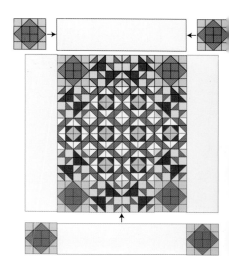

Our plan for this quilt was a gentle scheme of pale green and pink but we saw one of Moda's bright marble Jelly Rolls™ and you can guess the rest! The blocks were used in the Snowball Sampler Quilt and are great mixers, able to create good secondary patterns.

PEPPERMINT WHIRLS QUILT

VITAL STATISTICS

QUILT SIZE	54in x 54in
BLOCK SIZE	16in
BLOCKS PER QUILT	9 Blackford Beauty
SETTING	3 x 3 blocks + 3in wide border

REQUIREMENTS

- One Jelly Roll™ OR forty 2½in wide strips
- 26in (65cm) of fabric, cut into nine 2½in strips to become Colour C
- 24in (60cm) of border fabric, cut into six 3½in wide strips across the fabric width
- 20in (50cm) of binding fabric, cut into six 2½in wide strips across the fabric width

TOTAL STRIPS = 40½

- Nine blocks, which need 5½ strips each = 49½ strips.
- Less Colour C, which is replaced with extra fabric of 9 strips.

SORTING YOUR JELLY ROLL STRIPS

This quilt has just one repeated block. The calculations for our setting of three by three blocks showed that we needed 49½ strips, but don't panic, as even if additional strips are needed to make the quilt you have designed, there are ways to add extra fabric. We explain this here, to show just how adaptable the blocks can be in your Pick 'n' Mix quilts.

- From the Requirements for the Blackford Beauty block we can see we need 5½ strips per block and we want nine blocks in order to set it three blocks x three blocks. This means we need 49½ strips. To solve this there is nothing to stop us adding extra fabric. We have an amazing selection of forty fabrics already in the Jelly Roll™ so choosing an additional fabric is no problem. We just need to decide which fabric to replace. From the requirements for the Blackford Beauty block we can see that Colour C needs one Jelly Roll™ strip per block and, as we are making nine blocks, we can save nine Jelly Roll™ strips for the quilt if we replace Colour C with additional fabric. To calculate how much extra fabric is needed you must multiply 2½in by nine as we need to cut nine 2½in wide strips. This made 22½in exactly but we always allow just a little bit more which means we need 26in of additional fabric.
- So how do we find the extra half strip needed? We know that when making multiple blocks you often don't need quite so much fabric. For Colour D you only have to cut twelve 2½in squares per strip and we know by now that we can cut sixteen 2½in squares from one strip. There is our saving, so if we allocate Colour D half a strip less we will still have sufficient Jelly Roll™ strips.

This lovely quilt is made from just one repeated Blackford Beauty block, used in the Big and Bold Sampler Quilt. At first glance this quilt needs more strips than in a Jelly Roll™ but don't panic – crafty quilters always find ways around problems and we show you how.

MAKING THE QUILT

1 Follow the instructions in the Big and Bold Sampler Quilt for making the 16in Blackford Beauty block to make nine blocks in total.

2 Lay out the blocks as shown below and when you are happy with the layout sew the blocks into rows and then sew the rows together, pinning at every seam intersection to ensure a perfect match.

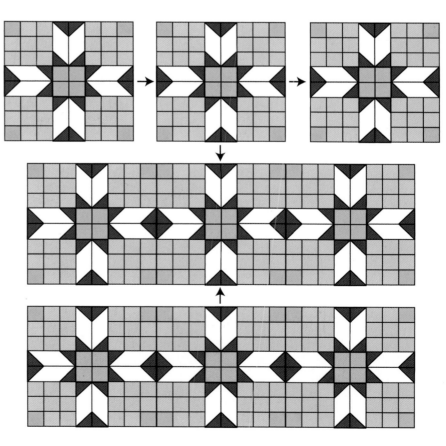

3 Sew the border strips into a one long, continuous
length and sew to the quilt – see Adding Borders
for instructions.

4 Your quilt top is now complete. Quilt as desired and
bind to finish – see Quilting and Binding a Quilt. A soft
aqua thread combined with a heart design was our choice to
finish this quilt.

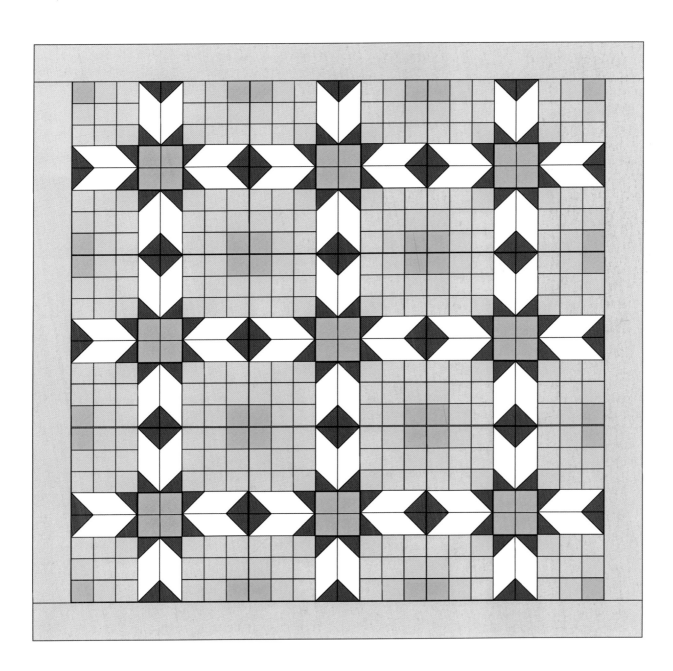

A QUARTER OF... QUILT

VITAL STATISTICS

QUILT SIZE 56in x 56in
BLOCK SIZES 16in, 12in and 8in
BLOCKS PER QUILT 4 Japanese Star, 4 Crow's Foot,
4 Love in the Mist and 4 Fan
SETTING 4 quarters, each of 7 block units

REQUIREMENTS

- One Jelly Roll™ OR forty 2½in wide strips
- 2¾yd (2.5m) of background fabric
- 20in (50cm) of binding fabric cut into six 2½in wide strips cut across the fabric width

TOTAL STRIPS = 39

- Four Japanese Star blocks of 6½ strips each = 26 strips. This includes 10 background strips so only 16 Jelly Roll™ strips are needed.
- Four Crow's Foot blocks of 2¾ strips each = 11 strips. This includes 4 background strips so only 7 Jelly Roll™ strips are needed.
- Four Love in the Mist blocks of 3¼ strips each = 13 strips. This includes 7 background strips so only 6 Jelly Roll™ strips are needed.
- Eight Fan blocks of 1½ strips each = 12 strips. This includes 6 background strips so only 6 Jelly Roll™ strips are needed.
- Four Flying Geese strips of 2 strips each = 8 strips. This includes 4 background strips so only 4 Jelly Roll™ strips are needed.
- Four four-patch units use up the last Jelly Roll™ strip plus offcuts.

SORTING YOUR JELLY ROLL STRIPS

- We replaced the background fabric in each block with cream strips. You can either choose to use the same cream throughout or create an even scrappier effect by using a neutral Jelly Roll™, which we did – and of course it saved time having the strips ready cut for us.
- When we got to the four-patch units, we had only one Jelly Roll™ strip left but never fear. There were plenty of offcuts and we easily managed to cut all the squares necessary for the four-patch units.
- Cut the background fabric into thirty-one 2½in wide strips and two 4½in wide strips cut across the fabric width.
- Subcut the 4½in strips into sixteen 4½in squares.

Remember years ago asking for a quarter of your favourite sweets? Perhaps this was the most important decision of the week – if only life stayed so simple! In this scrumptious quilt we have a collection of four different blocks –16in Japanese Star, 12in Crow's Foot, 12in Love in the Mist and 8in Fan. These are joined together with Flying Geese units and four-patch units to form a quarter of the quilt. Make four identical quarters and your quilt is made. It is also a very simple quilt to enlarge as you just need to make more 'quarters'.

MAKING THE QUILT

1 Follow the instructions in the Big and Bold Sampler Quilt for making the 16in Japanese Star block and make four in total.

Japanese Star block

2 Follow the instructions in the Star Sampler Quilt for making the 12in Love in the Mist block and make four in total.

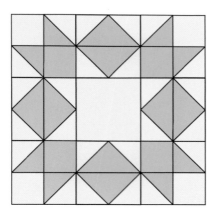

Love in the Mist block

3 Follow the instructions in the Star Sampler Quilt for making the 12in Crow's Foot block and make four in total.

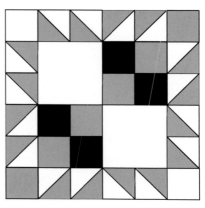

Crow's Foot block

4 Follow the instructions in the Snowball Sampler Quilt for making the 8in Fan block and make eight in total.

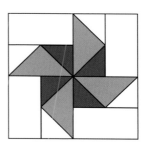

Fan block

5 Follow the instructions in Important Techniques to make thirty-two flying geese units. Sew four sets of eight together.

6 Sew four squares together to make a four-patch unit. Repeat to make eight four-patch units. Sew one to either side of a 4½in background square to form four four-patch rectangles.

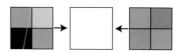

7 Sew the blocks together as shown in the diagram, right, to form one quarter of the quilt. Repeat to make four quarters and then sew the quarters together as shown below, rotating each quarter 90 degrees.

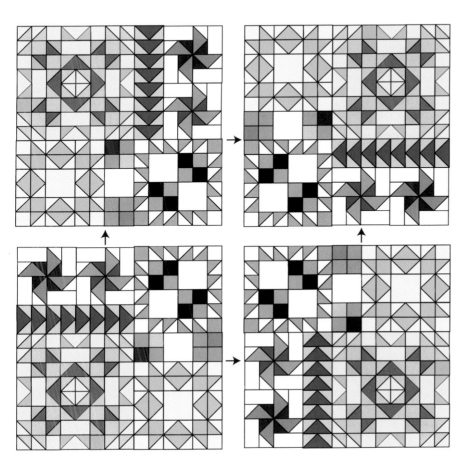

8 Your quilt top is now complete. Quilt as desired and bind to finish – see Quilting and Binding a Quilt. A simple meander design densely quilted seemed the perfect choice to finish this quilt.

GENERAL TECHNIQUES

TOOLS

All of the projects in this book require rotary cutting equipment. You will need a self-healing cutting mat at least 28in x 24in and a rotary cutter. We recommend the 45mm or 60mm diameter rotary cutter. Any rotary cutting work requires rulers and most people have a make they prefer. We like the Creative Grids rulers as their markings are clear, they do not slip on fabric and their Turn-a-Round facility is so useful when dealing with half-inch measurements. We recommend the 6½in x 24in as a basic ruler plus a large square no less than 12½in, which is handy for squaring up and making sure you are always cutting at right angles.

We have tried not to use too many different speciality rulers but when working with 2½in wide strips you do have to re-think some cutting procedures. You do need a speciality ruler to cut half-square triangles which you will find in a number of our quilts. Creative Grids have designed the Multi-Size 45/90 ruler for us, which enables you to cut both half-square and quarter-square triangles. This is perfect for our Jelly Roll™ sampler quilts. Whichever ruler you decide to use, please make sure you are lining up your work on the correct markings.

BASIC TOOL KIT

- Tape measure
- Rotary cutter
- Cutting ruler
- Cutting mat
- Needles
- Pins
- Scissors
- Pencil
- Fabric marker
- Iron
- Sewing machine

We quilters all have our favourite rulers. We like to use the Creative Grids rulers and squares, some of which are shown here, including the Multi-Size 45/90.

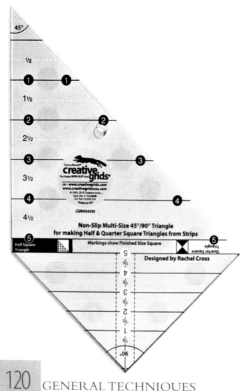

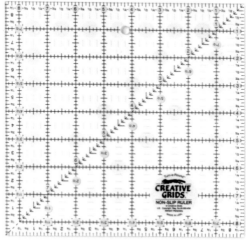

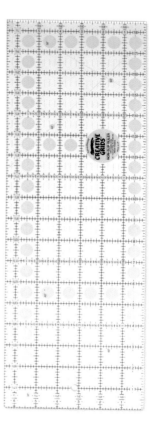

ROTARY CUTTING

Always take great care when using rotary cutting equipment as the blades are razor sharp. These instructions are for a right-handed person – reverse if you are left-handed.

1 Before cutting fabric with a rotary cutter the edge of the fabric must be straightened. Fold the fabric in half, selvedge to selvedge. Place the ruler along the right edge of the fabric, making sure one of the horizontal lines marked on the ruler is aligned with the fold of the fabric. This will ensure you are cutting at a right angle to the fold.

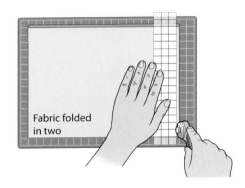

Fabric folded in two

2 Hold the ruler firmly with your left hand, positioning your thumb at the bottom of the ruler and your fingers stretching up the ruler but away from the edge. Hold the cutter in your right hand.

3 Keeping the blade against the edge of the ruler, push the cutter *away* from your body, stopping when the blade is level with your fingertips. Without lifting the cutter from the fabric, move the thumb on the ruler up to your fingertips and then move your fingertips up the ruler, walking your hand up the ruler as you continue cutting. This ensures you always have good pressure on the ruler so it does not slip.

4 Rotate the mat so that the ruler can still be held firmly with the left hand, you are now ready to cut strips, moving from left to right across the fabric. It is good practice to check that you are still cutting at a right angle after every four or five cuts. If you start cutting away from the right angle you will find that V-shapes will appear at the fold when your strip is opened out.

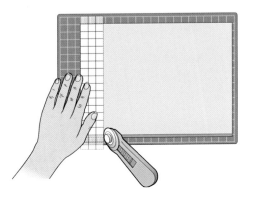

PRESSING

In quiltmaking, pressing is of vital importance and if extra care is taken you will be well rewarded. This is especially true when dealing with strips. If your strips start bowing and stretching you will lose accuracy.

• Always set your seam after sewing by pressing the seam as sewn, without opening up your strips. This eases any tension and prevents the seam line from distorting. Move the iron with an up and down motion, zigzagging along the seam rather than ironing down the length of the seam, which could cause distortion.

• Open up your strips and press on the right side of the fabric towards the darker fabric, if necessary guiding the seam underneath to make sure the seam is going in the right direction. Press with an up and down motion rather than along the length of the strip.

• Always take care if using steam and certainly don't use steam anywhere near a bias edge.
• When you are joining more than two strips together, press the seams after attaching each strip. You are far more likely to get bowing if you leave it until your strip unit is complete before pressing.
• Each seam must be pressed flat before another seam is sewn across it. Unless there is a special reason for not doing so, seams are pressed towards the darker fabric. The main criteria when joining seams is to have the seam allowances going in the opposite direction to each other as they then nest together without bulk. Your patchwork will lie flat and your seam intersections will be accurate.

PINNING

Don't underestimate the benefits of pinning. When you have to align a seam it is important to insert pins to stop any movement when sewing. Long, fine pins with flat heads are recommended as they will go through the layers of fabric easily and allow you to sew up to and over them.

Seams should always be pressed in opposite directions so they will nest together nicely. Insert a pin either at right angles or diagonally through the seam intersection ensuring that the seams are matching perfectly. When sewing, don't remove the pin too early as your fabric might shift and your seams will then not be perfectly aligned.

CHAIN PIECING

Chain piecing is the technique of feeding a series of pieces through the sewing machine without lifting the presser foot and without cutting the thread between each piece. Always chain piece when you can as it saves time and thread. Once your chain is complete simply snip the thread between the individual pieces.

When chain piecing shapes other than squares and rectangles it is sometimes preferable when finishing one shape, to lift the presser foot slightly and reposition on the next shape, still leaving the thread uncut.

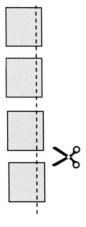

REMOVING DOG EARS

A dog ear is the excess piece of fabric that overlaps past the seam allowance when sewing triangles to other shapes. Dog ears should always be cut off to reduce bulk. They can be trimmed using a rotary cutter although snipping with small, sharp scissors is quicker. Make sure you are trimming the points parallel to the straight edge of the triangle.

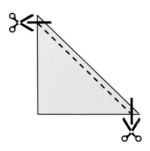

JOINING BORDER AND BINDING STRIPS

If you need to join strips for your borders and binding, you could join them with a diagonal seam to make them less noticeable. Press the seams open as shown.

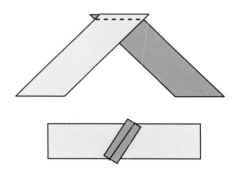

ADDING BORDERS

The fabric requirements in this book assume you are going to be sewing straight rather than mitred borders. If you intend to have mitred borders please add sufficient extra fabric for this.

ADDING STRAIGHT BORDERS

1 Determine the vertical measurement from top to bottom through the centre of your quilt top. Cut two side border strips to this measurement. Mark the halves and quarters of one quilt side and one border with pins. Placing right sides together and matching the pins, stitch the quilt and border together, easing the quilt side to fit where necessary. Repeat on the opposite side. Press open.

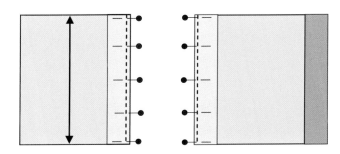

2 Now determine the horizontal measurement from side to side across the centre of the quilt top. Cut two top and bottom border strips to this measurement and add to the quilt top in the same manner.

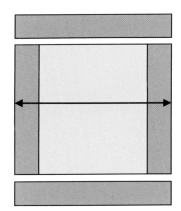

ADDING MITRED BORDERS

If you wish to have mitred borders rather than straight borders slightly more fabric will be required.

1 Measure the length and width of the quilt and cut two border strips the length of the quilt *plus* twice the width of the border. Cut two border strips the width of the quilt *plus* twice the width of the border.

2 Sew the border strips to the quilt beginning and ending ¼in away from the corners, backstitching to secure at either end. Begin your sewing right next to where you have finished sewing your previous border but ensure your stitching doesn't overlap. When you have sewn your four borders, press and lay the quilt out on a flat surface, with the reverse side of the quilt upwards.

3 Fold the top border up and align it with the side border. Press the resulting 45 degree line that starts at the ¼in stop and runs to the outside edge of the border.

4 Now lift the side border above the top border and fold it to align with the top border. Press it to create a 45 degree line. Repeat with all four corners.

5 Align the horizontal and vertical borders in one corner by folding the quilt diagonally and stitch along the pressed 45 degree line to form the mitre, back stitching at either end. Trim the excess border fabric ¼in from your sewn line. Repeat with the other three corners.

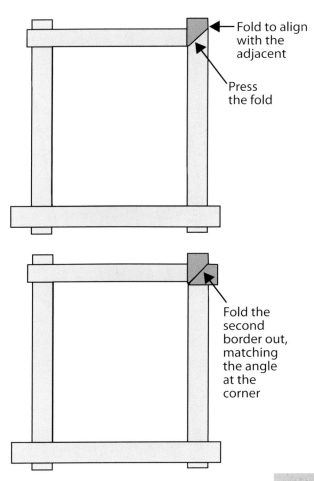

Fold to align with the adjacent

Press the fold

Fold the second border out, matching the angle at the corner

QUILTING

Quilting stitches hold the patchwork top, wadding (batting) and backing together and create texture over your finished patchwork. The choice is yours as to whether you hand quilt, machine quilt or send the quilt off to a longarm quilting service. There are many books on to the techniques of hand and machine quilting but the basic procedure is as follows.

1 With the aid of templates or a ruler, mark out the quilting lines on the patchwork top.

2 Cut the backing and wadding at least 3in larger all around than the patchwork top. Pin or tack (baste) the layers together to prepare them for quilting.

3 Quilt either by hand or by machine. Remove the marked lines and tacking on completion of the quilting.

BINDING A QUILT

The fabric requirements in this book are for a 2½in double-fold French binding cut on the straight of grain.

1 Trim the excess backing and wadding (batting) so that the edges are even with the top of the quilt.

2 Join your binding strips into a continuous length, making sure there is sufficient to go around the quilt plus 8in–10in for the corners and overlapping ends. With wrong sides together, press the binding in half lengthways. Fold and press under ½in to neaten the edge at the end where you will start sewing.

3 On the right side of the quilt and starting about 12in away from a corner, align the edges of the double thickness binding with the edge of the quilt so that the cut edges are towards the edges of the quilt. Pin to hold in place. Sew with a ¼in seam allowance, leaving the first inch open.

4 At the first corner, stop ¼in from the edge of the fabric and backstitch (see diagram A). Lift the needle and presser foot and fold the binding upwards (see B). Fold the binding again but downwards. Stitch from the edge to within ¼in from the next corner and repeat the turn (C). Continue all around the quilt working each corner in the same way. When you return to the starting point, cut the binding, fold under the cut edge and overlap at the starting point.

5 Fold the binding over to the back of the quilt and hand stitch in place, folding the binding at each corner to form a neat mitre.

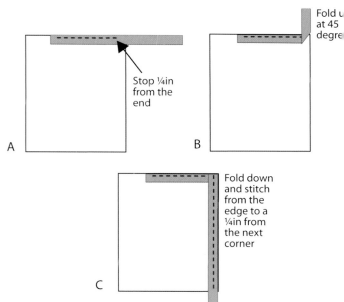

MAKING A LARGER QUILT

If you want to make a larger version of any of the quilts in the book, refer to the Vital Statistics of the quilt which gives the block size, the number of blocks, how the blocks are set plus the size border used. You can then calculate your requirements for a larger quilt.

SETTING ON POINT

Any block can take on a totally new look when set on point and you might like to try one of the quilts to see what it looks like on point. Some people are a little daunted as there are a few points to take into consideration but here is all you need to know.

How wide will my blocks be when set on point?

To calculate the measurement of the block from point to point multiply the size of the finished block by 1.414. Example: a 12in block will measure 12in x 1.414 which is 16.97in – just under 17in. Now you can calculate how many blocks you need for your quilt.

How do I piece blocks on point?

Piece rows diagonally, starting at a corner. Triangles have to be added to the end of each row before joining the rows and these are called setting triangles (see diagram, right).

How do I calculate what size setting triangles to cut?

Setting triangles form the outside of your quilt and need to have the straight grain on the outside edge to prevent stretching. To ensure this, these triangles are formed from quarter-square triangles, i.e., a square cut into four. The measurement for this is: Diagonal Block Size + 1¼in. Example: a 12in block (diagonal measurement approx. 17in) should be 18¼in.

Corners triangles are added last. They also need to have the outside edge on the straight grain so these should be cut from half-square triangles. To calculate the size of square to cut in half, divide the finished size of your block by 1.414 then add ⅞in. Example: a 12in block would be 12in divided by 1.414 = 8.49in + ⅞in (0.88) = 9.37in (or 9½in as it can be trimmed later).

Most diagonal quilts start off with one block and in each row thereafter the number of blocks increases by two. All rows contain an odd number of blocks. To calculate the quilt's finished size, count the number of diagonals across and multiply this by the diagonal measurement of the block. Do the same with the number of blocks down and multiply this by the diagonal measurement of the block.

If you want a rectangular quilt instead of a square one, count the number of blocks in the row that establishes the width and repeat that number in following rows until the desired length is established.

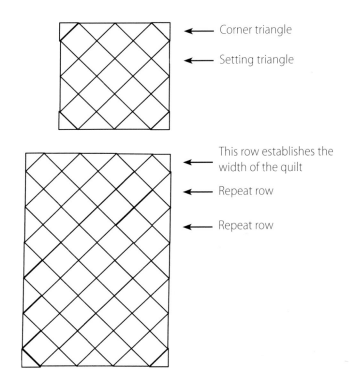

Corner triangle

Setting triangle

This row establishes the width of the quilt

Repeat row

Repeat row

CALCULATING BACKING FABRIC

The patterns in this book do not include fabric requirements for backing as many people like to use wide backing fabric so they do not have to have any joins.

USING 60IN WIDE FABRIC

This is a simple calculation as to how much fabric you need to buy. Example: your quilt is 54in x 72in. Your backing needs to be 3in larger all round so your backing measurement is 60in x 78in. If you have 60in wide backing, then you would buy the length which is 78in. However, if you have found 90in wide backing, you can turn it round and you would only have to buy the width of 60in.

USING 42IN WIDE FABRIC

For this width of backing you will need to have a join or joins in order to get the required measurement unless the backing measurement for your quilt is 42in or less on one side. If your backing measurement is less than 42in then you need only buy one length.

Using the previous example, if your backing measurement is 60in x 78in, you will have to have one seam somewhere in your backing. If you join two lengths of 42in fabric together your new fabric measurement will be 84in (less a little for the seam). This would be sufficient for the length of your quilt so you need to buy twice the width, i.e. 60in x 2 = 120in. Your seam will run horizontal.

If your quilt length is more than your new backing fabric measurement of 84in you will need to use the measurement of 84in for the width of your quilt and you will have to buy twice the length. Your seam will then run vertically.

LABELLING A QUILT

When you have finished your quilt it is important to label it even if the information you put on the label is just your name and the date. When looking at antique quilts it is always interesting to read information about the quilt, so you can be sure that any extra information you put on the label will be of immense interest to quilters of the future. For example, you could say why you made the quilt and who it was for, or for what special occasion.

Labels can be as ornate as you like, but a very simple and quick method is to write on a piece of calico with a permanent marker pen and then appliqué this to the back of your quilt.

ACKNOWLEDGMENTS

Pam and Nicky would like to thank Mark Dunn at Moda for his continued support and for allowing them to use the name Jelly Roll™ in the title and throughout the book. Thanks also go to Susan Rogers, Lissa Alexander and the rest of the team at Moda.

Thanks go to Bernina for very kindly allowing the use of one of their brilliant machines in the making of the quilts.

Thanks to the girls in The Quilt Room for their support and help in making several of the quilts. Thanks also to the members of Southill Piecemakers, Golberdon, Cornwall who are always ready to assist when time is short.

Last but not least, special thanks to Pam's husband Nick and to Nicky's husband Rob for their continued love and support – and we should say endless patience when the sewing machines are working overtime!

ABOUT THE AUTHORS

Pam Lintott opened her shop, The Quilt Room, in 1981, which she still runs today, along with her daughter Nicky. Pam is the author of *The Quilt Room Patchwork & Quilting Workshops*, as well as *The Quilter's Workbook.* Nicky now has the added responsibility of looking after Freddie who, at just over a year, is a great help in all aspects of quiltmaking! Pam and Nicky have now moved The Quilt Room shop back to its original roots where it first opened 30 years ago – into a reputedly haunted 15th century inn. They are waiting to find out if there are any ghostly quiltmakers around! *Jelly Roll Sampler Quilts* is Pam and Nicky's fifth book for David & Charles following on from *Layer Cake, Jelly Roll and Charm Quilts, Jelly Roll Inspirations, Two from One Jelly Roll Quilts* and their phenomenally successful *Jelly Roll Quilts*.

USEFUL CONTACTS

The Quilt Room
Shop and Mail Order
37–39 High Street, Dorking Surrey, RH4 1AR, UK
Tel: 01306 877307
www.quiltroom.co.uk

Moda Fabrics/United Notions
13800 Hutton Drive, Dallas, Texas 75234, USA
Tel: 800-527-9447
www.modafabrics.com

Winbourne Fabrics Ltd
(Moda's UK Distributor)
Unit 3A, Forge Way, Knypersley, Stoke on Trent ST8 7DN UK

Creative Grids (UK) Limited
Unit 1J, Peckleton Lane Business Park, Peckleton Lane, Peckleton, Leicester LE9 7RN, UK
Tel: 01455 828667
www.creativegrids.com

Sewmaster Sewing Machines of Reading and Guildford
Suppliers of Bernina sewing machines
www.sewmaster.co.uk

Bernina Sewing Machines
Tel: 020 7549 7868
www.bernina.co.uk

INDEX

Amish Star block 12, 75, 83
Arrowhead block 13, 18, 30

backing fabrics 126
Basket Sampler Quilt 6, 12, 13, 88–101
Big and Bold Sampler Quilt 6, 34–45
binding quilts 124
binding strips, joining 122
Blackford Beauty block 13, 34, 36, 42, 112–14
block frames 99
block library 12–13
    see also specific blocks
borders
    adding 32, 44, 70, 86, 123
    joining 122
    mitred 123
Buckeye Beauty block 13, 49, 55

Card Trick block 12, 14, 18, 28
Carpenter's Wheel block 12, 34, 36, 39
chain piecing 122
Chequered Star block 13, 34, 36, 41
Classic Sampler Quilt 6, 14–33
Connector block 13, 36, 43
corner units, flip-over 42, 98
Crow's Foot block 13, 75, 79, 116, 118
Cup and Saucer block 13, 75, 81
cutting 120, 121
    charts 18, 36, 49, 75, 91

dog ears, removal 122

Eccentric Star block 12, 49, 50
Eddystone Light block 13, 75, 82
Evening Star block 13, 49, 66

Fan block 12, 49, 60, 116, 118
Flying Dutchman block 13, 49, 57
flying geese units 12
    A Quarter of... Quilt 116, 118
    Big and Bold 38–41
    Classic Quilt 19, 23, 26–7, 29–30
    Snowball Quilt 50–1, 54, 57, 59–60, 64, 67
    Star Quilt 78, 80–5
four-patch units 30
Fox and Geese block 13, 49, 58, 110

Friendship Star block 13, 49, 53, 104, 106–7
Fruit Salad Quilt 104–7

Garden Trail block 13, 18, 27
Geese in Flight block 13, 49, 65

half-square triangle units 10, 92
    Big and Bold Quilt 38–40
    Classic Quilt 19, 20–2, 24, 26, 28
    Snowball Quilt 52–3, 55–6, 58–9, 61–3, 65–6
    Star Quilt 77, 79–81, 83–5

Indian Hatchet block 13, 75, 85

Japanese Star block 13, 34, 36, 40, 116, 118
jelly rolls 8
joining 122

Kaffe Fassett 34–44
King's Crown block 13, 49, 54, 110

labelling quilts 126
Liquorice Sticks Quilt 108–9
Love in the Mist block 12, 75, 84, 116, 118

Maple Star block 12, 14, 18, 29
Martha Washington Star block 12, 49, 67
measurements 8
Moda 8, 14, 33, 101, 110

Nelson's Victory block 13, 49, 64

Peppermint Whirls Quilt 112–15
pinning 122
pressing 121

Quarter of... Quilt, A 116–19
quarter-square triangle units 11, 25, 38, 41
quilting techniques 124

rail fence units 22
Railroad Crossing block 12, 34, 36, 38
Rhubarb and Custard Quilt 110–11

Rising Star block 13, 75, 80
Rocky Road block 12, 18, 20
Rolling Pinwheel block 13, 18, 23, 104, 106–7
Rolling Stone block 13, 18, 22, 108
rotary cutting 120, 121
rulers 120–1
    Multi-Size 45/90 10–11, 120

Sawtooth Star block 12, 49, 59
seams
    allowances 8, 12
    joining borders/binding strips 122
    pinning 122
    pressing 121
setting on a point 125
setting triangles 125
Shaded Trail block 13, 49, 63, 110
sizing quilts 8, 125
Snowball Sampler Quilt 6, 13, 46–71
Spinner block 13, 49, 56
Spinning Star block 13, 49, 52
Spiral block 13, 18, 26
Star Choice block 13, 18, 21
Star Sampler Quilt 6, 72–87
Stardust block 12, 75, 78
Streak of Lightning block 13, 14, 18, 31
strips
    joining 122
    sorting 8, 16, 36, 48, 74, 90, 104, 108, 112, 116

techniques 10–13, 120–6
tool kit 120
Tulip block 12, 18, 19, 108
Twinkling Star block 13, 75, 77

Union Square block 13, 18, 24–5

washing notes 8
Water Wheels block 13, 49, 61
Windblown Square block 12, 49, 51

X-Quartet block 49, 62